THE
HANDKNITTER'S
DESIGN BOOK

THE HANDKNITTER'S DESIGN BOOK

A Practical Guide
to Creating Beautiful Knitwear

ALISON ELLEN

David & Charles

Page 2: A jacket designed by the author, knitted in wool and rough silk by Louise Fisher

---

ABBREVIATIONS

K	knit	tog	together
P	purl	alt	alternate
C	cable	K1b	knit 1 into back of stitch
S	slip	P1b	purl 1 into back of stitch
Slp	slip 1 purlwise	psso	pass slipped stitch over
st	stitch	M1	Make one by picking up bar from row
st st	stocking stitch (knit 1 row, purl 1 row)		below
yf	yarn forward	beg	beginning
yb	yarn back	col	colour
yaf	yarn at front	cont	continue
yab	yarn at back	inc	increase
O or YO	yarn over needle (makes an extra st when worked in following row, leaving a hole)	dec	decrease

---

FABRIC CODING

><	pull in
△	pull up
<>	push out
[ ]	thick
O	open
/	bias
~	stretchy
—	flat (non-curling)
I	no stretch

A DAVID & CHARLES BOOK

Copyright © Alison Ellen, 1992
Photography by John Knight
First published 1992

A catalogue record for this book is available from the British Library.

ISBN 0 7153 9936 5

Typeset by ABM Typographics Hull
and printed in Italy by Milanostampa SpA
for David & Charles
Brunel House   Newton Abbot   Devon

CONTENTS

INTRODUCTION

Knitting is one of the most flexible ways of making fabric, in technique, colour and design – the possibilities for shape, texture and pattern are endless. If we can explore thoroughly what knitting can be made to do, we will be able to design and make something that has a special and unique quality.

This book is for knitters who enjoy experimenting with the colour and texture of yarns; and for those who would like to try designing and working their own patterns. Those who have not yet attempted to knit without a ready-made pattern may be surprised at how easy it can be, while more experienced knitters who already knit from their own designs will find helpful advice on the construction of different shapes, on the working out of details and on the finishing of garments.

It is always worthwhile taking the time to study traditional knitting methods – we only need look at the marvellous detail and rich patterning of jackets, hats, shawls and stockings indigenous to various parts of the world to appreciate how much we can learn from time-honoured, traditional handknitting techniques. Further, any serious knitter will want to investigate the character of knitted fabric, and how it is altered by the use of different yarns and stitches. So often we think of knitting simply as a way of making visual patterns, and tend to forget that those same stitches which form the pattern can also change the *feel* of the fabric, making it warm and substantial or light and cool, richly textured or smooth-surfaced, firm or flexible. All these things are considered, and we will see, too, how different combinations of yarns and stitches produce an infinite variety of knitted fabrics, ranging from fine shawls to warm jumpers, and from bedspreads to hearth-rugs.

Whole garments can be created, the shaping built into the construction by the use of different stitches, and the whole thing made in one piece, without seams; you can also dictate the way the fabric hangs or drapes by the direction of the knitting, whether it is worked vertically, horizontally, or on the bias. And it is always enormously satisfying to cast off the final stitches, having completed a tricky design by means of the knitting alone!

Colour is a crucial element in design. Some people have a natural talent for choosing the colours that will work most effectively together, but the process of noticing colour – in our surroundings, in works of art, in day-to-day design – can be learnt, so that it becomes a habit to analyse and make a note of particular colour combinations. This practice should help all of us when we build colour into our designs for knitting, the various shades intermingling as different stitches are introduced so as to produce an exceptional richness of pattern and texture. Those of you not already initiated might like to take a further step in exploring colour and try dyeing your own yarn, thereby enlarging your range and choice of colours even further and producing yet other effects in your knitted fabrics. The most efficient ways of knitting in several colours are discussed in detail, including intarsia and jacquard (or fairisle) knitting.

The **Stitch Library** is intended to help you choose the most appropriate stitches for any designs you might have in mind, and I hope it will also serve as a source of new ideas. It includes less frequently used stitches as well as the better known ones, though some of these are used in colour combinations that give them a completely new character. The Stitch Library is coded according to the character of the fabric created – whether it pulls in, pulls up, stretches or curls – and the codes can be used for quick reference when searching for a particular effect. Throughout the book, all the suggestions look for the *simplest* way of achieving each effect, both in design and construction, helping you, through a thorough understanding of the processes and materials involved, to use the flexible technique of handknitting to its maximum potential.

No book can produce your own original designs for you: it can tell you how to set about it, and make practical suggestions concerning technique and materials; and it can help to stimulate your imagination. Your own designs need not be ambitious or complicated, but must always be the product of your own ideas, your own observations, and your own experiments; and as I hope to have shown, anyone can have a go, and experience the enormous satisfaction of creating something individual.

The author at work in her studio

'Aunt Blanche': Newlyn, Penzance, Cornwall, c1902

1
Looking at
TRADITIONAL KNITTING

However eager you are to begin knitting your own designs, and to experiment with new ideas, colours, yarns and stitches, it is well worth stopping for a moment to look first at what was produced in handknitting in the past, and at what amazingly fine, detailed and rich work was created in times when making things by hand was the only way for people to clothe themselves, and furnish their houses.

The pace of life as we live it seems to accelerate as time goes on, and so also do our expectations for quick results, and instant and pre-packaged production. For many of us caught up in a way of life where time equals money, it is difficult to imagine spending the hours necessary to create just one garment or piece of fabric by hand, particularly when we know how quickly machines can operate. Looking at some of the exquisitely detailed handmade work from the past, it is hard to appreciate quite how much time has gone into the making process. The reasons for making things by hand have changed, too: no longer do we make because we *need* the finished product,

but simply because we want to be creative, with the satisfaction that is brought by using our hands. Quite recently the emphasis has also shifted: rather than taking great care to make something beautifully that will last, the aim seems to be to make an impact with an innovative design or use of colour.

Today we have a wide range of materials to choose from, whereas in the past, the choice of yarns and colours was limited to those available in each region. The extent of modern communication and travel means that we are exposed to an enormous range of design possibilities, both ancient and modern, and there is a lively exchange of ideas and influences in the design world, with pressure to be original and individual, within the bounds of fashion. This can be confusing, even overwhelming when trying to begin to design, in knitting or any other medium; but it is always inspiring and enlightening to look closely at work which was done when time did not have the same significance as it does today, and when the main priority was not speed of production.

A BRIEF HISTORY

If we look at craft objects made before this century they convey no sense of haste or urgency in construction, nor is there any sign of conscious effort to achieve new ideas and designs; but rather the detail, the finish and the fineness of much of the work gives a sense of calm and tranquillity.

The level of skill in all crafts has reached astonishing heights at different times in different parts of the world, but how well artefacts were preserved depended on the materials that were used, and the environment and atmosphere in which they happened to be. There are many examples of fine ceramics, metalwork, glass, and woodwork, but obviously textiles have not lasted as well as pottery or metalwork; the materials were not so durable, and fabrics were made to be used and worn. This was par-

ticularly the case with knitting, which was used at first for making everyday garments (usually underclothes), rather than clothes for special occasions, and these were often worn out! However, there is enough evidence remaining to trace knitted textiles a long way back.

Surviving fragments of textiles from different parts of the world demonstrate a wide variety of techniques, that must have been used for many hundreds of years. Although some of these resemble knitted fabric, they were in fact made by other means: they were often embroidered, as in needle knitting, which produced a surface resembling stocking stitch, but worked with a needle and thread; or they were made with netting; or with woven techniques such as Sprang, where threads are twisted round each other on a loom and produce a stretchy fabric,

■ Late 19th-century cotton lace knitting still held on the needles: this kind of edging would have been used to border a tablemat or cloth

again not unlike stocking stitch. The earliest known examples made on needles by the method we know as knitting have been found in Egypt and Spain. From these beginnings, the skill spread northwards, and there is later evidence of knitting throughout Europe, where it was in organised production from the Middle Ages onwards. It took a little longer to reach Britain, but there are examples of knitted stockings and hats, and references to knitting in Britain dating from Tudor times.

So we know that handknitting has been a part of everyday life in Britain and other European countries for several centuries. Further, it needs only a minimum of space and equipment to perform, and this might explain why it is one of the few native handcrafts in Britain that survived the industrial revolution as a commonly practised skill. Before this time spinning, weaving, and lace-making were cottage industries in various parts of the country; but together with crochet, knitting is the only structural textile technique (where the fabric is composed with a yarn, as compared with embroidery, which is worked

onto a ready-made fabric) that has continued as a widely accepted craft in the homes of ordinary people throughout the country to the present day.

During the 18th century knitting was the occupation of mainly working-class women, providing a useful income, or in some cases a supplementary income because they could knit whilst walking to and from work, waiting for the fishing boats to come in, or collecting fuel. There were also widespread cottage industries in stocking-knitting, which involved men as well as women; and around the coasts of Britain, of fishermen's 'frocks' or guernseys.

In the 19th century knitting began to be a fashionable pastime for ladies, whereas the cottage industry side gradually declined after the invention of knitting machines, both for stockings and other knitted garments.

In the early 20th century, two world wars created a different need for knitted clothes: socks, balaclavas and mittens were knitted by the dozen, and this probably helped to continue the general acceptance of knitting as a useful pastime for all classes of women.

More recently, in the last twenty-five years or so, there has been a tremendous resurgence of all sorts of crafts, including knitting, and handmade work has taken on an entirely new significance – though not always justifiably.

Looking at Traditional Knitting

Long before this 'modern' crafts movement became apparent, and weaving and knitting began to be designed and carried out by the new artist/designers, the production of various forms of handmade textiles had in fact been continuing all over the western world in a less self-conscious and more natural or 'ethnic' form. Sometimes this was as a craft for a particular trade – for instance, hand-weaving was an integral part of life in Scandinavia, and in remote corners of Britain such as the Scottish Isles; lace-making, braiding, crochet, knitting and netting continued in other European countries: and in England, at least until the 1940s and 1950s when it was still taught in schools, it was generally accepted that everyone could knit.

KNITTING PATTERNS

To begin with, knitting patterns would not have been written down, but copied by example from mother to daughter (or father to son in areas where men were the knitters), or shared whenever groups of women gathered together to knit and talk. Written knitting patterns have evolved more recently, and although there are examples of patterns as early as the 17th century, they were not commonly available until knitting became a more fashionable pastime in the early 19th century.

Speaking as someone brought up on knitting patterns who only after a training in textile design began to try to knit 'creatively', I believe that it is very easy to become brainwashed by knitting pattern jargon; line after line of 'K2 tog, P1, psso, S2,' and so on is not conducive to experiment, and the achievement in following a knitting pattern lies in making the jargon fit the stitches! Moreover the way British patterns are composed has a noticeable lack of information about the actual shape that is being produced. Continental patterns are rather more helpful in this, and use diagrams to explain shape and construction, whereas traditionally, British patterns lead one through a line-by-line maze and it is often a matter of luck if it all turns out right in the end! It takes quite a bit of knitting experience to be able to understand a knitting pattern on reading it through alone, and this blind following of written instruction does not encourage any inventiveness on the part of the knitter; nor does it make it easy to vary the stitch of the garment, let alone the shape.

So in order to be free to approach it creatively, let us start afresh, and consider knitting as though it were an entirely new technique for making a fabric.

■ A contemporary Peruvian hat and South American knitted doll, from the author's collection

BEGINNINGS OF KNITTING

It is interesting to try to imagine how knitting as we know it now might have begun all that time ago: it must have evolved originally from working with thread in the hand; forming loops and knots over the fingers, and gradually finding or making tools to help hook the thread through into loops. The thread continues without a break, forming new stitches into the loops below, on the needle, and building up a fabric that is essentially different from the best-known ancient textile technique of weaving in that it is elastic: it can stretch in every direction, although its greatest elasticity is widthways. This was (and still is) an enormous advantage for garments that needed to fit closely, for example 'hose' or stockings, vests and underclothes; and it makes a very comfortable fabric to wear in any form.

Another great advantage of this technique is that knitting can be shaped during the manufacturing process. While weaving creates rectangles or strips, in knitting, stitches can be picked up and knitted in any direction; flat or tubular pieces can be made, so garments of any shape can be made in one piece, often with no seaming.

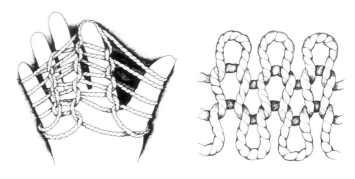

■ A form of the ancient game of Cat's Cradle, producing knitted loops over the fingers ■ The structure of stocking stitch *(right)*, which shows the way the yarn travels in loops, giving the fabric its characteristic stretchiness

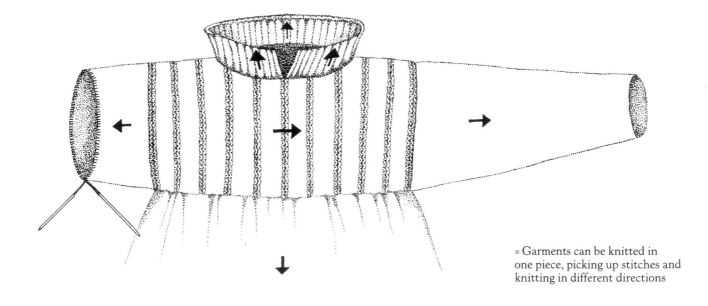

■ Garments can be knitted in one piece, picking up stitches and knitting in different directions

THE GUERNSEY

One garment that has kept its traditional method of construction and is still made today is the Channel Island guernsey, which is similar in shape to examples of knitted garments in the Victoria and Albert museum, such as the more ornate 'waistcoat' or undershirt in damask knitting worn by King Charles I. Fishermen's guernseys evolved from the knitted undershirts of the 17th and 18th centuries, in the course of time developing their own form of decoration, becoming thicker and more weatherproof; but the shape and construction did not need to change much over the centuries.

The way the guernsey is made is a good example of the most straightforward shape for a garment without seams: it is knitted as a straight tube with grafted shoulders, with narrowing tubes for sleeves, and a simple neck – but although it is such a simple shape, the stretch of the fabric enables it to fit differently shaped bodies without any special shaping or tailoring. If we study this basic shape first, it can lead on to more adventurous designs: shaping can be achieved within this method of making, to produce all sorts of variations in style and patterning, and any amount of decorative details.

A guernsey sweater, handknitted in the 1940s

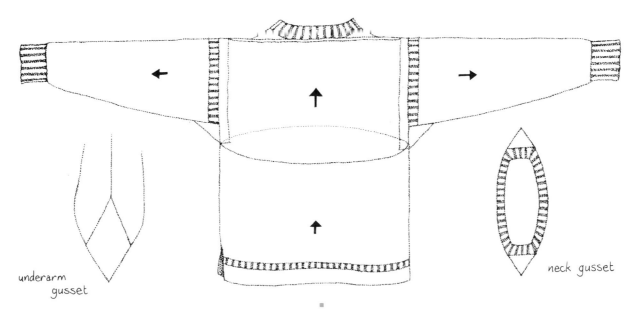

underarm
gusset

neck gusset

The construction of the traditional guernsey

TEXTURED PATTERNS

A great deal can be learnt from looking at examples of knitting from the past, and one might begin by considering just how much decoration and texture can be achieved by varied use of the different knitting stitches. Before the 19th century knitters did not have fancy yarns, and although dyes had been used for centuries, a lot of knitting was done in a plain yarn, without incorporating colour even for decoration. Probably the idea of colourful knitting did not arise while most knitted garments were used as underclothes. Now, we can create varied and colourful garments by using fancy textured and coloured yarns in no more than plain stocking stitch, whereas previously all decoration had to be achieved technically, by using different stitches.

Some of the early Dutch knitted garments in the Victoria and Albert Museum, London, show intricate patterning using just plain and purl stitches in undyed yarn, producing both geometric patterns and complicated floral designs which are very finely knitted, and truly beautiful when looked at closely. On a stocking stitch ground, a purl stitch will stand forward; and subtle differences in texture can be produced by using areas of purl-faced stocking stitch, and the rougher texture of moss stitch, against a knit-face ground.

More obvious textures and patterns are seen in examples of lace-knitting, cotton bedspreads, and Shetland shawls. As well as knit and purl, knitters made good use of decorative holes, arranging these to form innumerable patterns, fine and dainty in lace-knitting, or bolder in heavier knitted bedspreads. There are still plenty of examples in existence in museums, antique shops and private collections, showing elaborate patterning and some very fine-gauge knitting.

More heavily textured patterns were used by Austrian and also early Irish (Aran) knitters, where pronounced cable and cross-over patterns were used on a purl ground, often incorporating bobbles and embossed motifs; these give a richly textured surface.

KNITTING DESIGNS

Written instructions from the past can be a source of inspiration for designing, especially in patterns where stitches were used inventively. Knitting patterns from the first half of the 20th century, old knitting books, and early *Vogue* knitting patterns all show knitting stitches used for special effects of shaping and texture. These bring us into the field of fashion, where stitches are used consciously for styling as well as for decoration; but again, it is because there wasn't the choice of yarns we have now, that stitches were often more varied and elaborate than is usually found in patterns today.

WORKING CLOTHES

A different use of decorative stitches is evident in the early knitting of everyday working clothes, which often used decoration in a functional way. If a thicker fabric was needed, fancy stitches would be used to give a thicker texture. This could also be achieved by using more than one colour or yarn in places on the garment that were going to receive more wear, for example, necks and cuffs, welts and stocking heels. And the decorative yokes of fishermen's guernseys and Arans were so designed to give extra warmth where it was needed most, on the chest and back.

An unusual technique from Scandinavia called '2-strand' or 'twined knitting' was used in mittens and stockings, where two threads were used alternately, often in the same colour; so that although patterns are formed by carrying the spare thread at the front of the work to produce raised strands, it was evidently not primarily used for decoration, but for thickness and warmth.

Textured patterns

■ Cotton knitted lace and mats, from the author's collection

COLOUR
AND DECORATION

Until this century, the kind of patterning used in knitting would have been naturally well suited to the technique; decorative panels of coloured or textured stitches were usually placed horizontally, with small repeat patterns or motifs using diagonal or horizontal lines and blocks being very common; especially in colour knitting, where verticals, curves or circles are technically more difficult to achieve. Textured effects, especially cables, can easily be worked vertically in columns, as can be seen in early examples of Aran jerseys. But the approach was entirely different from the way we arrive at designs today. Now, we are governed by fashion rather than the technique of knitting; moreover any design or motif is possible, and acceptable.

Knitted clothes are designed (frequently not by knitters) as a whole 'effect', rather than worked row by row. This free approach is exciting and stimulating; but it is nonetheless very enlightening to see how much beautiful work was produced before designers were ever heard of, when the technique dictated the patterning.

TIME AND KNITTING
BY HAND

The time taken for hand-work also had a perspective different from today's understanding of it: as a result of mass production, we have come to expect instant results, and this has altered our attitude to things we do or make ourselves. Previously, hand-work was not expected to be fitted into odd moments and rushed through as quickly as possible. Fineness and intricacy were no object; the aim was to make things that would last and wear, and be handed on. Lace-making, embroidery, samplers, sewing or knitting would be 'sat at' for certain periods every day; and, as if looking through a magnifying glass (which was sometimes literally necessary), a little was done at a time, until the work was complete.

Knitting is one of the most flexible ways of making fabric, both in technique and because it uses the minimum of portable equipment, so that you are not tied to a particular place or machine for working. The possibilities for shape, texture and pattern are endless. However, it is important to examine the processes and the materials involved, so that we make best use of the knitting technique, by choosing the most suitable method and materials for each design or project. If we become familiar with this technique we can explore it and find out what knitting can be made to do, and make something that has a special quality through the particular construction of colour, pattern and texture created in the knitting process – rather than imposing a design which could just as well have been printed on to a jersey fabric.

A late 19th-century Shetland lace jumper knitted in
exceedingly fine handspun wool

2
The Character of
KNITTED FABRICS

Beginning with the basic materials, we will look at the different yarns available for knitting, and see how they knit up, then examine the various kinds of fabric that can be produced in knitting. The type of fabric produced by knitting is going to be affected by the stitch used, and also of course by the yarn. Knitting yarns are spun from a wide range of different fibres, some natural, some synthetic, and if we know a little about their characteristics, it will help us make the right choice of yarn for each design.

YARNS

Both plant and animal fibres are used for knitting yarns, and different fibres make very different types of yarn. Even the same fibre can make a variety of different threads, according to how it is spun. The character of the yarn is going to affect both the action of knitting and the finished product, so it is worth taking a closer look at how yarns vary, and how they might be expected to behave in knitting.

WOOL

The most widely used fibre for knitting is wool, which comes in an enormous variety of different forms. Woollen yarn can be bouncy, fluffy and warm; or sleek, smooth and shiny, as in worsted. It can be hairy, rough or soft according to the kind of sheep it comes from, and from which part of the fleece; the wool from the back and shoulders being much softer and finer than the 'britch' or rough outercoat on the legs and haunches. Some of the

toughest, roughest wool comes, predictably, from hardy, mountain breeds of sheep such as the Herdwick and Swaledale; and the softest yarns from sheep of gentler climates, for example the Merino. So within the range of wool yarns alone there is scope for fine knitting, using warm, soft, or sleek and smooth wools; and for making a heavier, coarser fabric using thicker, rougher wool. However, the general characteristics of all wool yarns are, firstly, that it has a natural 'give' or elasticity which makes it easy to handle and work with (although this does vary according to the spin, worsted yarns being smoother and less stretchy); and secondly, wool is always warm to wear, although to differing degrees.

Commercially produced knitting wools are often prepared for knitting by blending with synthetic fibres, or by treating to reduce the felting properties, making it easier to wash without shrinkage. However, some of the character of the fibre is occasionally lost in this process, and it is worth searching for a supply of 'whole' wool if you would like to experiment and see how it knits by comparison with treated yarn. It often has more spring, or life in it, taking up the shape of the knitted stitches in a more vigorous way. Some suppliers of weaving yarns have wools which look and feel very different from knitting wools, and which knit beautifully; these also wash well if treated carefully (see List of Suppliers).

The choice of yarn also depends on what use the proposed garment will receive: for example, children's clothes will obviously need more washing than an adult's jacket or cardigan, and this must be taken into account when deciding on yarn.

Natural yarns for knitting *(left)*. Numbers refer to yarn tags in foreground.

1 & 2 not visible	*12* white alpaca
3 wool	*13* silk/alpaca
4 worsted-spun wool	*14* silk noile
5 English Britch	*15* tussah silk
6 Falkland Island wool	*16* spun silk
7 Herdwick	*17* soft-spun cotton
8 as 7	*18* mercerised cotton
9 Icelandic wool	*19* indigo-dyed plain cotton
10 coarse alpaca	*20* linen
11 soft alpaca	

The Character of Knitted Fabrics

LUXURY FIBRES

Some lesser known animal breeds give more exotic yarns. Of the llama family, alpaca is one of the best known; it produces a long-fibred yarn which hangs quite limply, and is known best for its soft and lustrous character, although much of the fleece is in fact very coarse. As these animals are becoming more popular to keep domestically, the fibre is more readily available, although still quite expensive (see List of Suppliers).

Angora and Cashmere are breeds of goat producing fibre for luxury yarns: the Angora is well known for the fluffy nature of its wool, known as mohair; and the Cashmere produces a very soft, fine yarn, taken from combings from the softest part of the fleece. It is often expensive, but combines well with wool or silk to make a luxurious yarn.

Even rabbit hair can be used for knitting, with the incredibly soft angora being the most popular: again, it blends well with wool.

COTTON AND LINEN

Vegetable fibres such as cotton and linen make yarns with virtually no stretch at all, unless spun as a fancy yarn, for example a bouclé; and they can be difficult to knit with. They are harder on the hands; and as they are not fluffy, they will show every stitch clearly (including irregularities in the knitting). However, textured stitch patterns are shown to their best advantage in plain cotton and linen yarns: even subtle patterns in plain and purl show up well (see chapter 1, cotton bedspreads p14).

They hang differently from wool: cotton, for example, is surprisingly heavy and hangs in a more relaxed, lifeless way than wool. But although dramatically different in every way from wool, cotton and linen have valuable qualities of their own. They feel cool to wear, and although so much heavier than wool of the same thickness, can be used successfully as very fine yarns. As they are not springy, there is less tendency for the knitting to curl up, so they are well suited to knitted mats, spreads or cloths that need to lie flat. The weight and drape of a cotton knitted bedspread is quite distinctive and gives a marvellous soft, heavy, cool feel that could not be achieved in any other material.

Cotton is spun in a wide variety of yarns: the plainest and cheapest have a matt finish, ranging from dishcloth cotton to something a little more sophisticated. Fabric knitted in these yarns has to be washed carefully to prevent shrinking or stretching, although this can be helped to a certain extent by choosing a firm stitch that will keep its shape. The most practical cotton for knitting with is mercerised cotton which has been treated to increase its strength and improve its dyeing qualities; this process gives the yarn a nice sheen, and it wears well without losing its shape. Cotton is also spun into fancy and textured yarns such as bouclé, and is often combined with synthetics to improve washing ability and to make a less heavy yarn. However, a good cotton, if knitted in a suitable stitch and at the right tension, will wear well, and will probably wash by machine.

Linen has its own different qualities. First, it can make an extremely fine, strong yarn, hence its traditional use in lace-making – the fineness of the thread used when the lace industry was at its height is still incomparable. Second, linen has a natural sheen to it, when finished and pressed; and it displays a light, flexible drape, unlike the weightiness of cotton. On the other hand it is inclined to show every crease, although it can be blended with various fibres to make this less noticeable. In the past it was woven with wool to make 'linsey-woolsey' cloth; but nowadays the linen-mix yarns available are more likely to be blended with cotton or synthetics.

SILK

Silk is surprisingly warm, and although difficult to use on its own – some silk yarns can lose their shape and become limp – it combines well with wool, either in a wool/silk mix yarn, or used as a separate thread in a jacquard or slip-stitch pattern with wool (cashmere, alpaca) or cotton. Again, there is a variety to choose from, from smooth shiny reeled silks, to spun silks, and rougher silk noiles. There is more choice from mail order suppliers than High Street retailers (see List of Suppliers).

SYNTHETICS

The choice of yarns available today for knitting is enormous, and it is very easy to be attracted by colour rather than character; but as we have seen, every yarn behaves differently. Synthetic fibres are added to help with the washing properties of natural yarns, as well as being made into yarns in their own right. They can imitate some of the qualities mentioned above, but one of the main differences between natural and synthetic yarns is their ageing and wearing properties. This might seem an unusual aspect to worry about, but if one is taking the time and trouble to knit a beautiful garment or furnishing fabric, and it is going to be kept and used for as long as possible, it is worth considering how it will look when it has been around for a while! Natural fibres become old and worn out, like everything else, but they do it gracefully, and an old piece of silk has more beauty than worn nylon or acrylic. Certainly, a percentage of nylon will make a yarn more hard-wearing; but if you enjoy using natural yarns, why not try and use a knitting technique to make a more hard-wearing cuff or welt? Choose an appropriate stitch to give a stronger fabric; use a double thread to reinforce, as in the knotted-edge method for guernseys (this also makes a very decorative edge, see chapter 3, sample on p38); or knit sleeves, and even welts, downwards, so they can be unpicked and re-knitted easily when they have become thin and worn.

OTHER MATERIALS

You do not have to use conventional yarns, or bought yarns for knitting. Handspun yarns will produce knitted fabric with a different look and feel, and are available from some craft fairs, shops, or Guilds of Weavers, Spinners and Dyers (see List of Suppliers). It is satisfying to use a yarn that has not been through the stress of a machine process, but has been manufactured by hand throughout. One point to look out for when using a handspun yarn is that the amount of twist in the spinning occasionally causes the knitted fabric to slant sideways. Usually this only happens if the yarn is a single unplied strand, but it can also occur if there is too much twist in the plying; it is important therefore to knit a sample first.

Try knitting with completely different materials, for example ribbon, string, rags, polythene; think of unusual materials for knitted bags, cushions, floor rugs: there are potential supplies in all sorts of unexpected places – hardware shops, garden centres – perhaps even waste packaging.

Rags provide a lot of scope for knitting: again, the choice of fabrics is limitless; and patterned fabrics will give different effects from plain colours. If cloth is cut into strips on the bias, it will have some stretch in it, which makes it easier to knit with, and there is less tendency to fray. Very fine rags can be knitted into garments, and heavyweight strips could be used for knitted rugs.

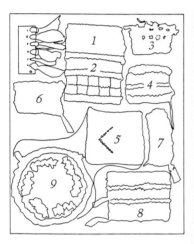

■ Alternative materials for knitting:
1 linen string
2 Icelandic wool
3 raffia
4 handspun wool (beginner's spinning)
5 linen
6 plastic carrier bag, cut into strips
7 cotton rag
8 cotton rag
9 wool rag

STRETCH

The main characteristic that makes knitting different from most other structural textile techniques has already been mentioned: namely its stretch. Crochet is the closest relative to knitting, but does not have so much elasticity because the loops are continually being laid over each other (as in casting-off), which prevents them stretching out to their full width. Some of the fun and challenge in designing with knitting is in how the amount of stretch can be varied, and the fabric made more, or less elastic according to the stitch used.

Knitted fabric can be as open as netting; as light, trans-parent and decorative as lace. The stitches can be fine, or coarse and open; or at the other extreme, close, tight and thick like woven cloth, to the point where there is almost no stretch.

BEHAVIOUR OF DIFFERENT STITCHES

When designing a garment, remember that the sort of stitch used is going to affect the feel and hang of the knitting, as well as the look, texture and pattern. This is often ignored in knitting patterns, or only referred to by a

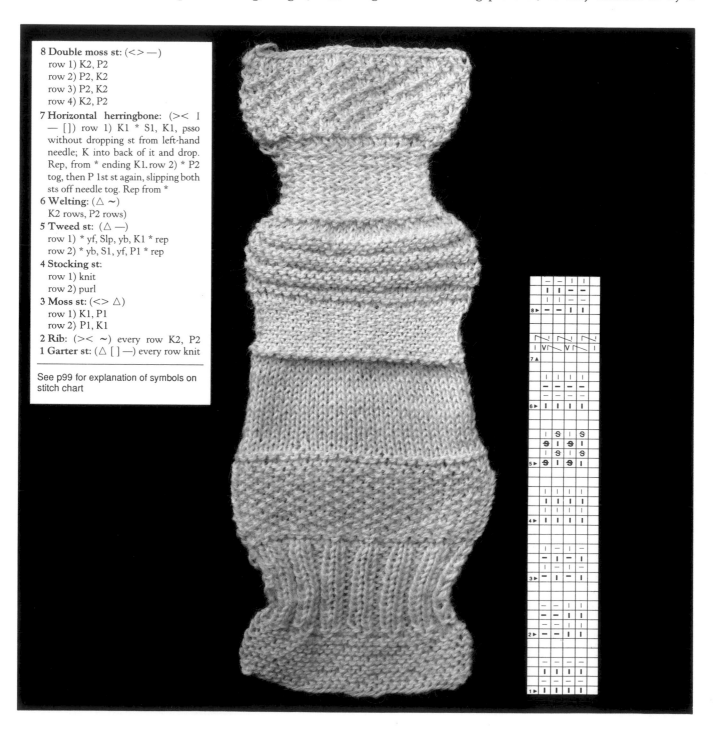

8 Double moss st: (<> —)
row 1) K2, P2
row 2) P2, K2
row 3) P2, K2
row 4) K2, P2

7 Horizontal herringbone: (>< I — [ ]) row 1) K1 * S1, K1, psso without dropping st from left-hand needle; K into back of it and drop. Rep, from * ending K1. row 2) * P2 tog, then P 1st st again, slipping both sts off needle tog. Rep from *

6 Welting: (△ ~)
K2 rows, P2 rows)

5 Tweed st: (△ —)
row 1) * yf, Slp, yb, K1 * rep
row 2) * yb, S1, yf, P1 * rep

4 Stocking st:
row 1) knit
row 2) purl

3 Moss st: (<> △)
row 1) K1, P1
row 2) P1, K1

2 Rib: (>< ~) every row K2, P2

1 Garter st: (△ [ ] —) every row knit

See p99 for explanation of symbols on stitch chart

general description of the yarn type: ie chunky, supersoft, and so on. However, if you are designing your own pattern, a particular stitch cannot be chosen simply for its look without considering the weight or drape, the thickness, or the amount it will pull in, or spread out. If this is ignored, it could result in surprises and disappointments. (See Stitch Library coding, for how different stitches behave).

COMPARING STRETCH IN DIFFERENT STITCHES

The most commonly used stitch is stocking stitch, which also gives the plainest, smoothest fabric; so it makes a useful basis for comparison with other stitches, if knitted in a sample with equal numbers of stitches and rows. Stocking stitch has more rows than stitches to a square, ie each stitch is wider than it is tall. There are several stitches that pull in more than stocking stitch, but few that are wider. Moss stitch is an example of a wider one, where the knit and purl stitches push away from each other sideways, and pull up vertically, making fewer stitches and more rows than in an equivalent sample of stocking stitch.

In the two sample strips shown here, 14 rows are worked of each pattern, on 28 sts and the same needles throughout, separated by a K-2-row ridge between each pattern.

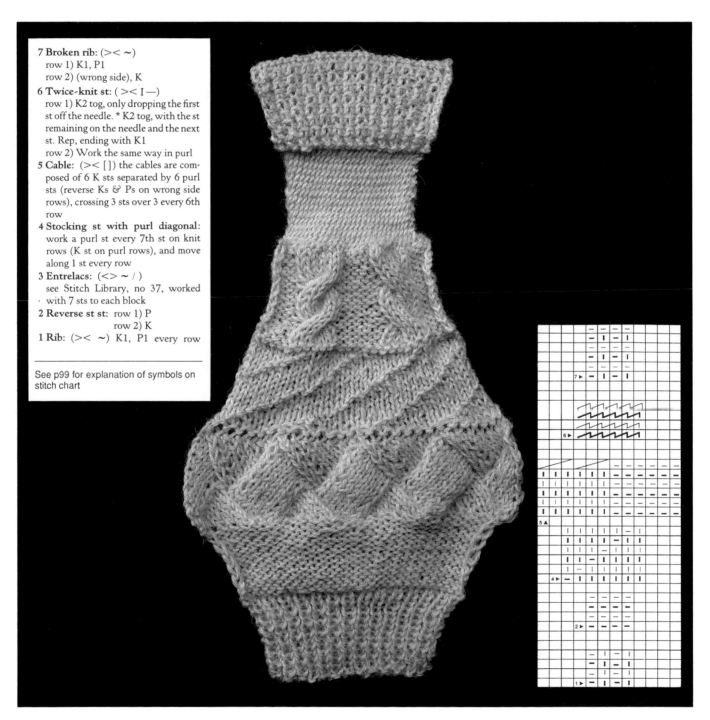

7 Broken rib: (>< ~)
   row 1) K1, P1
   row 2) (wrong side), K

6 Twice-knit st: (>< I —)
   row 1) K2 tog, only dropping the first st off the needle. * K2 tog, with the st remaining on the needle and the next st. Rep, ending with K1
   row 2) Work the same way in purl

5 Cable: (>< [ ]) the cables are composed of 6 K sts separated by 6 purl sts (reverse Ks & Ps on wrong side rows), crossing 3 sts over 3 every 6th row

4 Stocking st with purl diagonal: work a purl st every 7th st on knit rows (K st on purl rows), and move along 1 st every row

3 Entrelacs: (<> ~ /)
   see Stitch Library, no 37, worked with 7 sts to each block

2 Reverse st st: row 1) P
                     row 2) K

1 Rib: (>< ~) K1, P1 every row

See p99 for explanation of symbols on stitch chart

FLAT STITCHES

Together with stretch, and the amount of pull-in and pull-up that different stitches have, another important factor to consider in the way stitches affect the fabric is whether they will cause it to lie flat or curl up.

The most commonly-used stitch, stocking stitch, has a tendency to curl at the edges. It curls purl-side out at the top and bottom of the knitting, and knit-side out at the sides; as will all stitches with a predominence of knit one side and purl the other. The type of yarn used and the amount of twist on the yarn will make a difference to this, some curling more than others; but any stitch of this type will need another stitch as an edging to prevent curling (unless the curling is incorporated into the design: see chapter 7 p90).

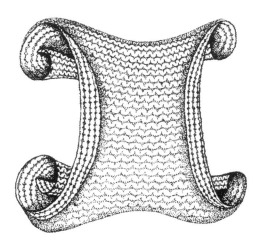

The nature of stocking stitch fabric is to curl purl-side out at the top and bottom edges, and knit-side out at the side edges.

In order to produce a fabric that lies flat, the pattern needs to have either equal stitches of knit and purl, ie rib; or equal rows of knit and purl, ie garter stitch or welting. Most flat stitches can be used as an edging to stocking stitch: the alternative is to knit a 'double cloth', ie knit-side showing both sides, either by knitting and slipping alternate stitches to make a double fabric (see Stitch Library), or to knit a facing, which counteracts the curl when it is sewn back on the inside.

It is worth noting that ribbing in two colours does not behave like single-colour rib as it has no elasticity, but is more like a stocking stitch. This is because the tension produced by changing from knit to purl in a single yarn – which makes the fabric buckle, pushing the knit stitch forward and the purl back to form the ribbing – does not happen when the yarn is changed at this point. So it flattens out like stocking stitch, and therefore may curl at the edges (again depending on the yarn). If it is used as a welt, it might need a plain stocking-stitch facing knitted (using a needle one size smaller) to counteract the curl; in this way, it makes a strong, reliable edging.

EDGINGS

The character of the stitch is vital in cuffs and welts, as these are the finished edges and need to be firm. Generally, we need elastic borders that can be stretched over heads and that will pull back in again to hold the garment in shape. Ribbing is so successful at this that it is used almost exclusively for welts, in variations of K1, P1, or K2, P2; but there are other elastic stitches that could be used for a change, eg spiral ribbing, or rib alternating with other stitches; or welting used sideways. On jackets, however, where necks and welts do not have to be stretched over the body, a firm edging could be used which need not be elastic, but must be depended upon

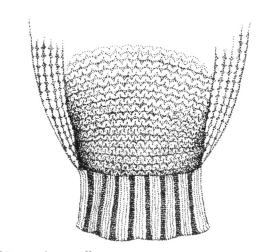

Ribbing used as a cuff

A welt with stocking-stitch facing

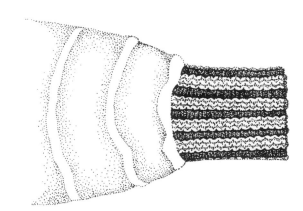

'Welting' (K2 rows, P2 rows), knitted as a cuff

not to lose its shape. This gives scope for unusual edgings, and less commonly-used firm stitches could be tried to give a decorative finish, eg cross-over and cabled stitches; 'woven' stitches; or twice-knit stitches (see Stitch Library, and chapter 7).

Not only will some less-stretchy stitches provide strong welts, they will also make wonderfully warm and firm fabrics for larger garments such as coats and jackets, that will keep their shape without drooping; since a stitch with less 'give' is less likely to sag and lose its shape.

DRAPE

The next question is, how will the knitting hang, or drape, when it is made into a large piece? Again, yarn will have an important part to play in this, but so will the stitch that is used, and the direction in which it hangs. A piece of plain stocking stitch will hang differently when used vertically or horizontally, or on the bias.

SIDEWAYS

We have already found that knitting has more stretch sideways, so it follows that if a large jacket or jumper is knitted in a fairly loose tension and heavy yarn, working across the garment from cuff to cuff, it will be inclined to sag, stretch and grow. But there are several ways of counteracting this tendency, by careful choice of stitch.

Colour knitting in the form of fairisle or jacquard, or slip-stitch patterns will help, because the strands of un-knitted colour travelling on the back will inhibit stretch. (Note that intarsia will not work in the same way, because the colours do not travel across the whole width of the knitting.)

Cabling or any cross-over stitch will also help to pull in the width and prevent stretching; as, to some extent, will simply twisting the stitches by knitting or purling into the backs, as this prevents the stitch pulling out to its full width. The main advantage to using knitting 'on its side' in this way would be to give an overall effect of vertical patterning, as it is much easier to knit colour patterns horizontally and use them sideways, than to knit colours in a vertical pattern (see chapter 4).

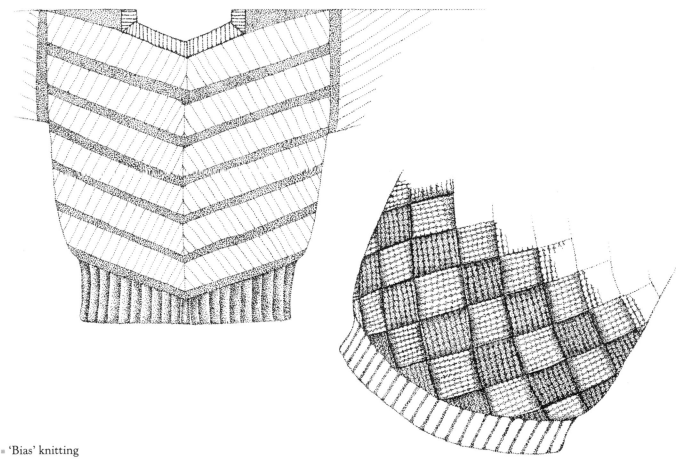

■ 'Bias' knitting

'Sunflower' jacket by Sarah Burnett, knitted in jacquard across
the garment so that the pattern falls in vertical bands

The Character of Knitted Fabrics

BIAS KNITTING

Bias knitting is different again; it behaves rather like woven fabric used on the bias in that it drapes well, has more all-round stretch, and feels flattering and comfortable to wear. There are many different ways of achieving a bias direction in knitting:

▪ By increasing at one end of a row and decreasing at the other, which keeps the number of stitches constant but slants them diagonally.

▪ Stitches can be increased and decreased at various regular points within the row, which will slant the stitches towards a diagonal, in a zig-zag form. On a small scale, traditional stitches such as 'Old Shale' and other zig-zag stitches (see Stitch Library no 31) have small sections between the increases and decreases which form continuous strips of bias fabric. On a larger scale, increases and decreases placed at wider intervals will make a garment shape dip up and down, and will have the same effect of slanting the stitches to the diagonal.

▪ Perhaps the most obvious bias knitting is produced by entrelac stitches (sometimes called 'basket-weave'), where diagonal rectangles are worked one at a time in rows, but joined in to the previous row as they are knitted. Again, this can be worked on a small scale in little rectangles, or in very large rectangles that fill the garment. It makes a fabric that hangs very well, feels good to wear, and is not difficult to knit – although word-by-word instructions are essential the first time you try it, until you see how it works (see Stitch Library no 37).

Working out sizing in this stitch is complicated (see chapter 7): depending on the scale of the rectangles, either the number of rectangles can be changed, or the number of stitches in each rectangle can be altered.

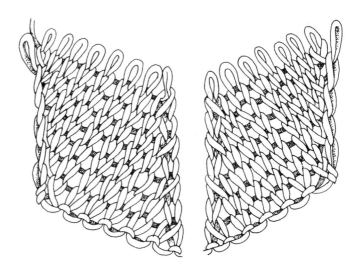

▪ Bias knitting, showing increases and decreases to produce a zig-zag fabric

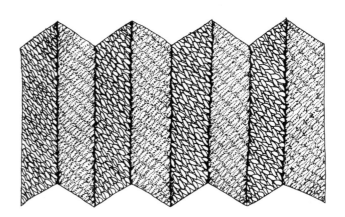

3

KNITTING TECHNIQUES

EQUIPMENT

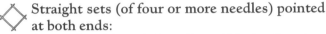

One of the advantages of handknitting is that the equipment needed is minimal and portable. There are basically three different types of knitting needle available:

Straight 'pins' with closed ends:
With two straight needles you can knit two-dimensional pieces of knitting of virtually any shape from one corner or end to another.

Straight sets (of four or more needles) pointed at both ends:
A set of double-ended needles will knit a flat piece beginning at a centre point; or will knit a tube of any diameter, from the smallest possible of one stitch per needle, upwards, according to the length and number of needles.

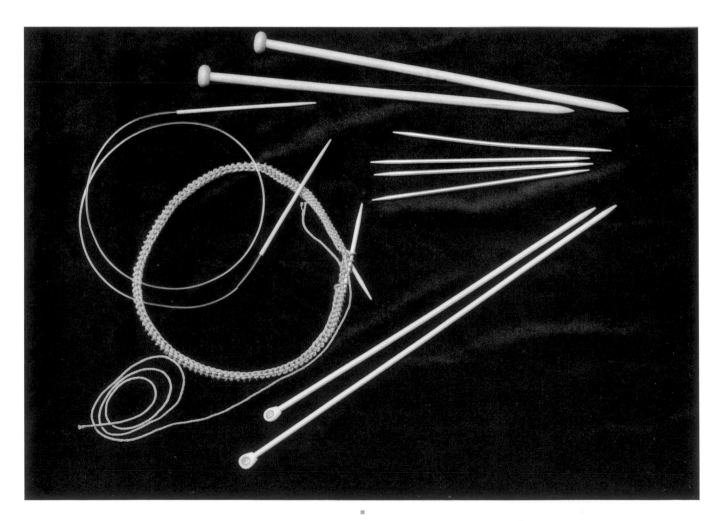

Types of knitting needle: straight 'pins' in steel or wood, a set of double-ended steel needles, and circular needles in steel and bamboo

Circular needles (sometimes called 'twinpins'). These have normal rigid ends to hold and knit with, joined by a length of nylon which can vary in length. Circular needles will knit back and forth like two needles to produce 2-D knitting, or will knit tubes with the circumference ranging from the length of the needle upwards, but not smaller than the length of the needle. The shortest circular needles available are designed for knitting necks. These also have shorter rigid ends than the longer sizes, which makes them more awkward to hold, and it may be preferable to use a set of four needles for small circumferences.

CHOOSING NEEDLES

There are times when one sort of needle is more appropriate than another, and the advantages and disadvantages of each type in relation to certain projects, are listed below:

KNITTING A JUMPER

Two straight needles will knit flat pieces that need sewing together.

A set of needles can knit in the round, but using several needles at a time can be cumbersome.

A circular needle is ideal for tubular knitting, and no seams are necessary. Note: always use a needle slightly shorter than the circumference of the garment, as the stitches can crowd comfortably onto the needle, but cannot be stretched round a needle that is too long.

KNITTING A JACKET

With two needles, knit in separate pieces and sew together.

As for the jumper above, using sets of needles is not really appropriate.

A circular needle will knit the width of the whole jacket back and forth with no side seams, and the length of the needle can be used to spread out the whole width, to inspect the knitting as it progresses. If very wide, spread out on two circular needles.

▪ A circular needle can be used for knitting in the round, and back and forth across a whole garment, with a short circular needle used as a stitch-holder

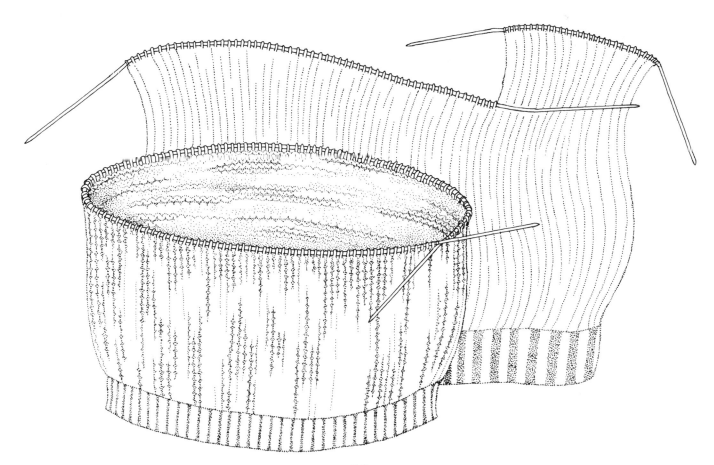

Knitting Techniques

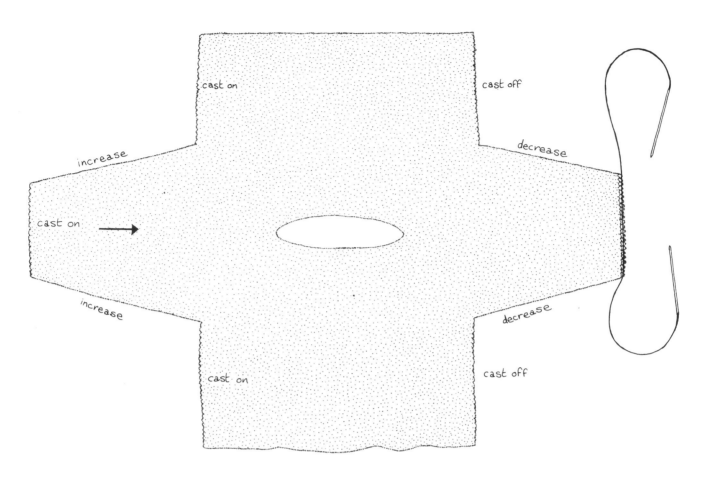

■ Jumpers and jackets can be knitted from cuff to cuff on circular needles

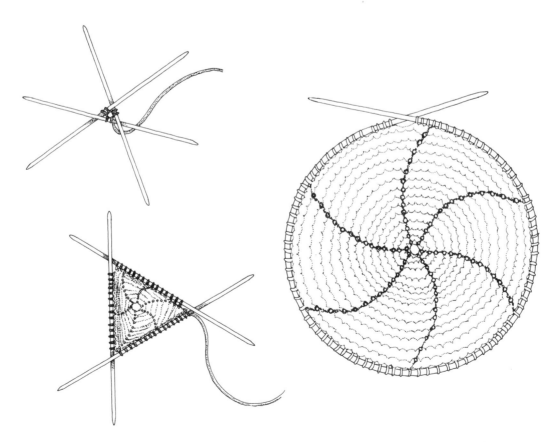

■ Knitting from a centre point in circular knitting, beginning on a set of double-ended needles and progressing to a circular needle when there are enough stitches

JUMPERS/JACKETS
KNITTED FROM CUFF TO CUFF

On two needles, the width of knitting would be limited by the length of needle, so a shoulder seam might be needed.

Sets of needles: not really appropriate.

Again, circular needles will accommodate a large amount of stitches, so a garment could be knitted back and forth, cuff to cuff, with no seam on the shoulders.

KNITTING FROM A CENTRE POINT, IN
CIRCULAR KNITTING

Two needles: not appropriate.

Sets of needles are ideal here; work with at least three needles holding the stitches, knitting with a fourth; and one or two sts on each needle, increasing sts on subsequent rounds.

Circular needles: only possible when there are enough sts to fit length of circular needle. A flat circular piece would need to begin on a set of needles (as above), and progress onto a circular needle when enough stitches have been increased. Oval shapes could be knitted by casting on minimum stitches that will fit the needle, then increasing with sets of needles in two main areas (at each end of the oval) and sewing the gap together afterwards, in a straight line.

ODD-NUMBER ROWS OF COLOURS

Using two needles, yarn will be at wrong end of needle when needed, so not appropriate.

On double-ended needles, stitches can be slid back to other end of needle, and the row knitted in the same direction again.

On a circular needle, treat as double-ended needles if knitting back and forth; or if knitting in the round, each colour will be at the beginning of the round whenever needed.

■ Odd-number rows of colour, knitted on a double-ended needle

STOCKING STITCH

On two needles: 1 row knit, 1 row purl.

On a set of needles, if working in the round, all knit.

On a circular needle, if working in the round, all knit. Sometimes, particularly in colour knitting, it is useful not to have to purl, and always to have the right side facing you.

FINE STRIPES OF COLOUR

Knitting on two needles: stripes can be matched when joining pieces.

Sets of needles: not appropriate.

Circular needles: not appropriate, because spiral knitting will cause stripes to step at the colour change (this step is not so noticeable in wide stripes).

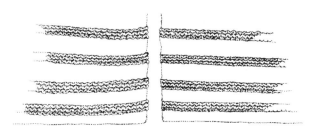

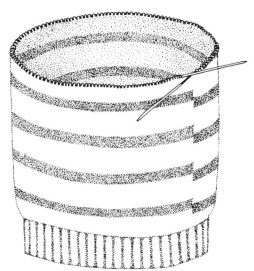

■ Fine stripes of colour do not meet up in circular knitting, but can be matched in a seam

NEEDLES USED AS STITCH-HOLDERS

Pairs of needles are not appropriate.

Sets of needles are not appropriate.

Circular needles make good stitch-holders, as stitches do not easily fall off.

INTARSIA

Two needles are suitable.

Sets of needles are not appropriate.

Circular needles: it is not possible to knit intarsia in the round, as yarn will be the wrong end of each colour section on the next round.

To sum up, circular needles are very versatile as they can knit in the round as well as back and forth, and they make successful stitch-holders. The advantages of knitting without seams are great, and will be described later (see chapter 7). As we have already seen, there are only a few instances when circular needles are not appropriate: when knitting from a centre point in circular knitting; in fine stripes of colour, when there will be a step at the colour change; and in intarsia, which is not possible to knit in the round (see above).

POSITION OF HANDS IN KNITTING

If you are going to do much knitting, you must be comfortable: it should be relaxing! First, look at the way you sit: check whether you are tensing your shoulders or neck, and whether your back is properly supported. Now look at the position of your hands: are they tensed to grip the needles or the yarn? If you get an aching neck, back or hands after a period of knitting, it would be worth examining the way you knit.

HOLDING THE NEEDLES

There have always been differing opinions about the best way to hold the needles and the yarn in knitting. Different people prefer different positions, and find it very hard to change; it is always difficult to break a habit, and frustrating to lose fluency through using a new hand position. But in order to gain the maximum speed with the minimum of work for the knitter, the fingers need to be near to the tips of the needles, so the yarn has the shortest possible journey to make round the needle.

This can be done most easily if the needles are held on top, rather than underneath like a pen, so that the fingers are free to move forward with the yarn. This applies to circular and straight needles alike – the more freedom the hands have in order to work the yarn over the needle, the quicker the action.

If the weight of the knitting is supported, the hands are free to knit more easily. In the past, a knitting sheath might have been worn on a belt, and the end of the needle inserted into it, leaving the hands with more freedom. If using straight needles, it would be worth trying a knitting sheath (see List of Suppliers) to see if you can knit with more speed in this way. Because circular needles do not stick out sideways, the weight falls more centrally on to the lap, so the problem is not quite the same; although a large garment does become heavy if knitted in one piece.

Holding knitting needles:
a) on top of the needle,
b) like a pen

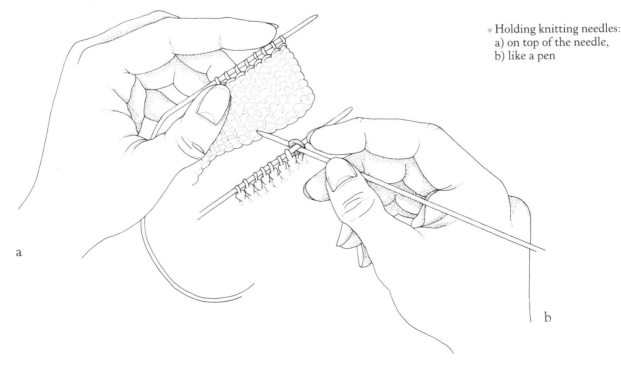

a

b

HOLDING THE YARN

There are traditional variations throughout the world in the way yarn is held for knitting: in Britain, it is held predominantly in the right hand; in Germany and some Scandinavian countries, it is held in the left. Traditionally in Portugal and South America the yarn is passed once round the neck to keep it under tension, and not held with the hand at all, but lifted over the stitches with the left thumb.

The yarn-in-left-hand, or 'continental' method, is easier and speedier for knit stitches, as the yarn does not have to travel round the needle, but is in the correct position to be picked up by the tip of the right needle. This also applies to changing from knit to purl within a row, as the yarn can slip between the needles from front to back or vice versa without having to reach round the point of the right-hand needle, making rib- or moss-type stitches much quicker. Left-handed purl is a little more complicated, but no slower than right-handed.

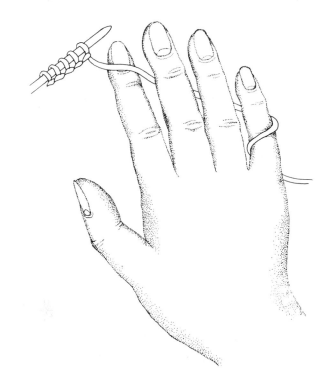

▪ Holding the yarn, twisting once round the little finger to give tension

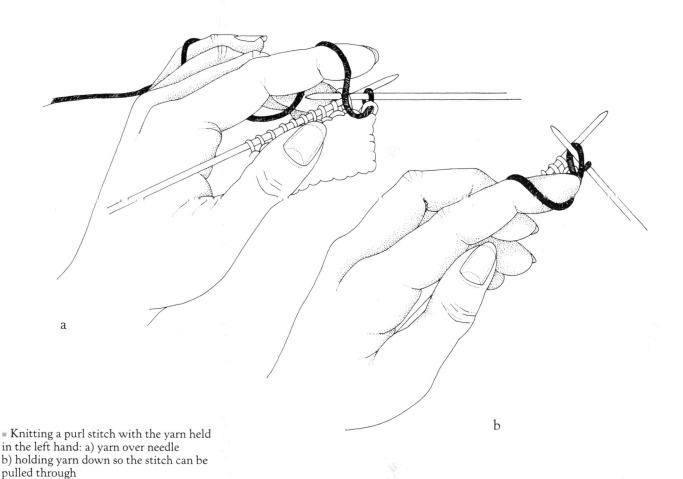

a

b

▪ Knitting a purl stitch with the yarn held in the left hand: a) yarn over needle
b) holding yarn down so the stitch can be pulled through

Ideally, both right- and left-handed methods are useful, because when knitting with more than one colour, one can be knitted in one hand and one in the other, and yarns do not have to be dropped and picked up but are always ready to knit, and do not become tangled. It can become almost as fast as knitting in a single colour.

In both hands, the yarn needs to be twisted once round the little finger to give it tension, so it does not have to be grasped tightly.

If you are starting from scratch, or feeling adventurous, it would also be useful to learn to knit in 'mirror image', or 'knitting back backwards', ie knitting stitches from the right-hand needle to the left. Thus by knitting one row in 'normal' knitting and the next in 'mirror image', the work would not have to be turned, but would always have the right side facing you (as in circular knitting); so in this case there would be no need to purl to produce stocking stitch: every row would be knit. This is especially useful when working in short-row patterns, such as bobbles or entrelacs, where turning the knitting constantly is cumbersome and awkward; knitting back backwards over the same small group of stitches saves time.

The action is not quite the same as normal knitting: the left-hand needle is inserted into the *back* of the first stitch on the right-hand needle, and the yarn wrapped over the *top* of the left needle. This produces a stitch ready to knit in the normal way in the next row, without twisting.

TENSION

It is always essential to test out the tension of your knitting by making a sample. If you are designing your own pattern, you must be able to calculate how many stitches you will need, and you have to measure the number of stitches and rows per centimetre in a sample before you can work this out. If you are following a pattern, it will not come out the size expected unless your tension is the same as that stated.

If you are trying out a new way of holding the needles or yarn, your tension may be different until you get used to it, so check your tension as soon as you feel comfortable knitting.

Sometimes tension can alter, too, so that the tension in the knitting of a small sample is different from that in a large garment on a circular needle, with the increased weight of the fabric. Some people also discover that they have a different tension for knit and purl, which will certainly make a noticeable difference if you are knitting stocking stitch in the round, then changing to working back and forth, and introducing purl rows (ie above the armholes). You have to be aware of the way you knit, and make adjustments if some stitches come out looser than others. Try and aim at the stitches fitting comfortably on the needle without being too loose, whatever stitch is being knitted.

If the knitting is uniformly either loose or tight, it is very easy to alter the general tension of single-colour knitting by changing the needle size; although this does not always apply to jacquard knitting.

TENSION IN COLOUR KNITTING

Knitting in jacquard or fairisle can produce different tension problems, because it is usually the yarn travelling at the back that is affecting the width rather than the needle size. Although a bigger needle will make a bigger stitch, if the other yarns are too tight, the stitch will still be restricted widthways and will appear longer, rather than wider. The only remedy here is to examine your technique, and see if you can hold the yarn not being knitted in a more relaxed way. A piece of knitting with a good, even tension should feel relaxed, with no strain or tightness, but with no floppy, uneven looseness, either.

SAMPLES

It is tempting to consider sampling a waste of time and yarn, but in the end it can save both time and mistakes. If you are experimenting with ideas in your samples, these can be pinned up somewhere for you to look at, and can be very decorative. Living with your trial pieces in this way often leads on to new ideas, as you are seeing them from close up and from a distance. They could also be joined together in a patchwork 'sampler' which could then be made into a cushion or bedspread. Don't unpick samples and throw them away; they are always useful for reference, even if only to remember what not to do!

It is essential to mark samples with a note about the stitch used, and the needle size.

■ Knitting with the yarn held in the left hand

CASTING ON AND OFF

A piece of knitting can be spoiled by weak selvedges, or it can be given a professional finish by good, strong, neat edges. There are several ways of making all the selvedges in knitting, both the cast-on and cast-off edges, and the side edges; and it is worth experimenting to see how they differ, and to decide which one would be appropriate for each project or design.

CASTING ON

Some methods of casting on are more generally useful than others; some are more suitable for a particular purpose. Cast-on edges can also be made decorative by the use of a contrasting colour.

There are more ways of casting on than casting off, and in order to decide which type of edging to use when designing a garment or furnishing, you have to consider what kind of characteristics are needed. For example:

- Does it need to be a thick, strong edge? ie on a jumper, jacket, coat, rug, blanket. (See Stitch Library.)
- Does it need to be neat, professional, and preferably unnoticeable? ie fine knitted garments, tailored, classic styles; baby garments, lace knitting, plain ribbing.
- Perhaps elasticity is the most important factor? ie close-fitting jumpers, garments for children.
- Does it need to be strong and non-stretchy? ie jackets, cushions, coats.
- If you can't decide how to begin, or what sort of welt to use on a garment, then a provisional cast-on would be useful, so that stitches can be picked up and the welt knitted later.
- If it needs to match the cast-off edge, ie on a garment knitted cuff to cuff, use the crochet-hook method (see sample 9) to give an identical edge.

CASTING OFF

This is more restricted by the fact that the knitted loops have to be laid over each other to fasten off securely, and there are fewer ways of accomplishing this than in casting on. Because each stitch is being looped over its neighbour, the stitches are no longer able to stretch out fully, so there is a tendency for a cast-off edge to be tight. However, there are still ways of varying this edge.

The method of casting off that we know best (see sample 1) gives a horizontal line at the edge, which is not always sympathetic to the pattern of the fabric knitted. It can be emphasised and made into a decorative feature by using a contrasting colour; or, the look of the cast-off edge can be softened by casting off 'K2 tog' (see sample 2) which also sometimes eases the tension, even though the loops are still being laid over each other.

The first of these cast-off edges is much quicker to do using a crochet hook, and the 'K2 tog' method is easier with knitting needles.

The most decorative cast-off edge is picot, which is also much more elastic, as the 'picot points' give the finished edge a longer surface area.

These are the most useful methods of casting off, although all sorts of variations are possible using a crochet hook (refer to Bibliograpy).

SIDE EDGES

The side selvedge of a piece of knitting is also very important to the look of the fabric, and a piece of knitting can be spoiled by poor edges. This is more noticeable if it is going to be left unattached, but a wobbly edge also makes a weak seam, whether it is sewn, or is going to have stitches picked up from it.

Side edges can be avoided by circular knitting, which makes a tubular fabric. This also saves having to sew up afterwards, and is preferable in all cases except those listed earlier (knitting from a centre point; fine stripes; intarsia) when the stitch used is unsuitable.

Methods:
- The first stitch of every row is worked in pattern (knit or purl, according to pattern). This makes a firm edge, but depends on even knitting. If the purl stitch is looser than the knit, the edge will be uneven, and often a piece of stocking-stitch fabric has one edge looser than the other for this reason.
- The first stitch of every row can be slipped; this gives a 'chain' effect, as the edge stitch is stretching over two rows. It makes a neat edge if the selvedge is being left unjoined. It is also useful in entrelacs stitch, as it leaves clear loops which are picked up and knitted in another direction.
- A feature can be made of the edges by knitting the first and last two stitches of every row, giving a little garter-stitch strip. Garter stitch is inclined to pull up lengthways, and so will help keep the edges firm.
- If more than one colour is being used, as in jacquard, the other colour(s) *must* be woven *right* to the edge. If they are not carried right across, the last few stitches will be weaker and thinner than the rest of the knitting, which is disastrous either as an edge or a seam. If the jacquard stitch uses both knit and purl, ie 2 & 2 rib in two colours, and the second colour cannot be woven to the edge (see colour knitting p55), it is still worth stranding the second colour to the edge, very carefully, without pulling; and twisting round the other yarn at the end of the row, so that the correct thickness is maintained right to the edge.

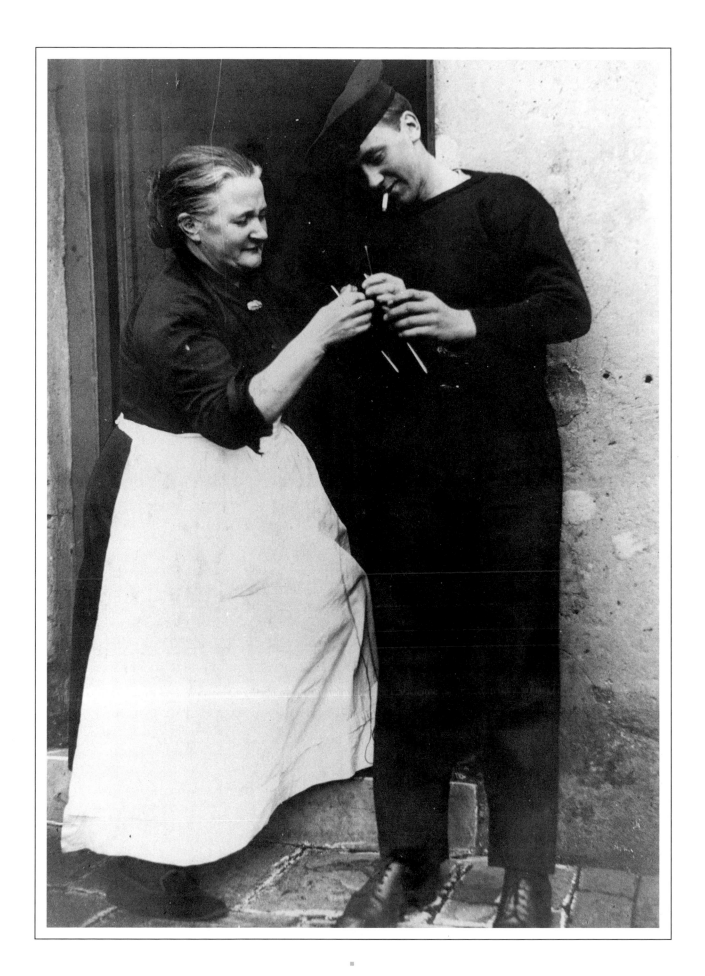

Knitting on Tyneside

■ 1) Knit-on cast-on, knit and cast off

■ 2) Cable cast-on, K-2-tog cast-off

■ 3) Single thumb-twist cast-on, purl cast-off

■ 4) Thumb-twist with two ends

■ 5) Thumb-twist purl cast-on

■ 6) Picot-point cast-on and off

■ 7) Knotted-edge cast-on

■ 8) Knotted-edge, with knots in contrast colour

■ 9) Cast-off cast-on

■ 10) Provisional cast-on
K-2-tog cast-off

■ 11) Invisible cast-on

1 KNIT-ON CAST-ON

a) make a slip-loop onto LH needle
b) insert RH needle into loop and make a st
c) instead of slipping LH st off, put RH st onto LH needle; rep b & c

This can make a rather loose, loopy edge, although the loops could be used for picking up and knitting downwards.

KNIT AND CAST OFF

a) knit 2 sts
b) using the tip of the LH needle, lift the first st on RH needle over the last-knitted
c) knit another st, and repeat from b

This is the most commonly-used form of casting off, giving a neat chain edge with very little stretch. For a quicker method, use a crochet hook instead of the RH needle, and work single crochet which casts all stitches off.

2 'CABLE' CAST-ON

Begin as in (1), but when 2 sts are made, * insert RH needle between the 2 sts, make a new st, and put back onto LH needle. Rep from *.

This makes a firm edge, with not very much stretch.

K-2-TOG CAST-OFF

K 2 tog, place Rh st onto LH needle; rep
This makes a cast-off edge which looks quite different from (1), although it is no more stretchy as the loops are still being laid over each other; but here they go from left to right in pairs, instead of from right to left in a chain.

3 SINGLE THUMB-TWIST CAST-ON

a) make a slip loop on RH needle
b) twist yarn over L thumb by starting with the thumb above the yarn, and place on RH needle, rep

This edge is tight to knit on the following row, but has the advantage of working along the RH needle in the same direction as the knitting, so is useful for buttonholes, or the bell frill (see Stitch Library), where it is necessary to cast on in the middle of a row.

PURL CAST-OFF

As (1), but purling instead of knitting.

4 THUMB-TWIST WITH TWO ENDS

Make a slip-knot some way along the yarn, leaving a tail end, which is used as in (3) for the thumb-twist. Insert the RH needle into the loop on the thumb and knit it with the main yarn to make sts.

This makes a strong, elastic edging. When the next row is knitted (working back and forth), the purl side will be showing as a 'ridge'.

5 THUMB-TWIST PURL CAST-ON

Exactly the same as above, but purling the st off the thumb, so that when it is turned to make the following row, the knit (smooth) side is facing.

6 PICOT-POINT CAST-ON

This is made as picot-point chain, picking up the sts along the edge of the chain.
a) make a slip-loop on LH needle
b) knit-on cast-on (see (1)) to make 2 more sts
c) knit and cast off (see (1)) until 1 st left
d) put RH st back on LH needle, and rep from b

2 sts are picked up from each 'point', so cast on half as many points as sts needed.
This cast-on is best used with a flat-lying stitch rather than a gathering or ribbed edging.

PICOT-POINT CAST-OFF

a) Knit and cast off 3 sts
b) * put last RH st back on LH needle, and work as for picot-point cast-on b & c, then cast off 3 more normally, and repeat from *

The number cast off between the points can be altered to make them closer or more spaced out.
Both these edges are elastic, and decorative.

7 KNOTTED-EDGE CAST-ON
(Channel Islands method)

Make a slip-knot on RH needle some way along the thread, as the tail end is used double.
a) twist the doubled end twice round the L thumb, beginning with the thumb under the yarn (in opposite direction to nos (3) & (4)), and knit through both loops to make a st on RH needle with the single (main) yarn; pulling double yarn through carefully until firm.
b) place single yarn over RH needle
c) Rep a & b, and in following row knit both a and b sts: b makes extra sts which help space out the knotted sts.

This makes a neat edge if worked with thickish yarn on fine needles, and is not suitable for a gathering stitch: ie use with garter st rather than ribbing. It is very strong, stretchy, and can be decorative.

8 CONTRAST-COLOUR KNOTTED EDGE

As 7, but contrast colour is used for double thumb knots only; the stitches are knitted in main colour.

9 CAST-OFF CAST-ON

a) make a slip-loop onto LH needle
b) holding yarn in left hand, use a crochet hook in RH, insert hook into loop and make a st, keeping it on the hook
c) place crochet hook over needle, and pick up yarn, pulling through to make a st over the needle
d) pass yarn round so it is below needle again, and rep from c

The last st is transferred from the crochet hook to the needle.
This makes a firm chain edge, identical to method 1 cast-off edge.

10 PROVISIONAL CAST-ON

a) make slip-loop on RH needle in main yarn. Use a contrast yarn to run under the needle to hold the sts, keeping end firm by tucking it into RH
b) place main yarn over L thumb, and contrast yarn over L forefinger
c) main yarn makes sts by passing over the needle always from the front to the back, alternately (i) enclosing contrast yarn by passing under it and round the needle, and (ii) twisting with it by coming in front and underneath it, then passing over needle

Contrast yarn should be kept firm, and lie in a straight line under the needle.
When the sts are knitted in the first row, loops will be left on the contrast yarn, and can be picked up later and knitted downwards, removing the contrast thread.
Cast-off: K2 tog in contrast colour (see 2).

11 INVISIBLE CAST-ON

For use with K1, P1 rib, or with tubular (double) knitting. Make a slip-loop on LH needle, and cast on a 2nd st.
a) * insert RH needle from the back to the front between these last 2 sts
b) take the yarn round the needle as if to purl, and draw the yarn through onto the RH needle, taking care not to twist it as it is placed on LH needle
c) insert the RH needle from front to back between the last 2 sts on the LH needle
d) take the yarn round the needle as if to knit, and draw the yarn through onto the RH needle, taking care not to twist it as it is placed on LH needle; continue from * until required no of sts are made

For ribbing: with an odd no of sts, begin the next row with a P st: with an even no, begin with K.
On first row, work into back of loop of each K st.
This makes a very tidy, professional-looking edge, with no hard line: the ribbing starts from the very edge.

PICKING UP STITCHES

Stitches can be picked up from anywhere on a piece of knitting and knitted in another direction, either from the side or bottom edge (for sleeves or front bands), or from the middle of the work (for motifs, tucks, pockets, or also for decoration).

WHAT TO PICK UP

If the selvedge is strong there should be no problem picking up the edge stitches, but it is important not to pick up weak loops or holes. As the knitted stitch is wider than it is tall, on a stocking-stitch fabric you need to pick up fewer stitches than there are loops (rows) available: the general proportion of stitches to rows is 3 stitches to every 4 rows. (This applies to plain stocking stitch only; different stitches will pull in or pull up more: see chapter 7 for how to work out the correct number of stitches.)

If the selvedge is weak or loopy, it may be necessary to pick up stitches *not* from the edge, but one or two stitches in. This does not make such a smooth seam as the edge stitches will leave a ridge inside, but it is preferable to picking up stitches from weak loops.

■ Picking up stitches from the edge of the knitting

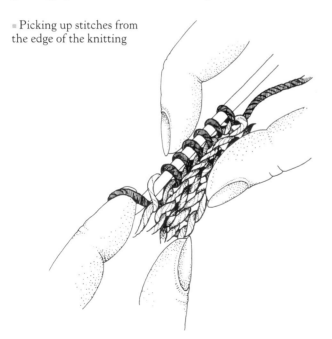

HOW MANY STITCHES TO PICK UP

There are two essential points to get right in picking up stitches:

1 Check your tension to calculate the correct number of stitches to pick up.

If you are using the same sized needles to pick up with, and knitting in the same pattern and tension as before,

your tension measurement can be taken from the main piece of knitting – for example, if you are picking up round an armhole to knit a sleeve downwards, you are probably knitting the same fabric as before. But if you are knitting on in a different tension, for example front bands knitted sideways on smaller needles, it is essential to knit a sample to measure the tension, using the smaller needles.

CALCULATING FROM A TENSION SAMPLE

a) measure 10cm across your sample, and count the stitches.
b) measure the length of the piece you want to pick up from: *but* if this is a side edge, measure a little way in from the edge, as the edge is often looser than the body of the knitting.
c) To calculate the number of stitches to pick up, divide the required length measurement by the sample measurement (ie 10cm) and multiply by the number of stitches in the sample.

ie required measurement ÷ 10cm × no of sts in sample

---

2 Pick them up evenly: ie the same number at one end of the row as at the other. Stitches grouped unevenly can spoil the shape of a whole garment.
Mark the piece you are picking up from with pins or safety pins, first at the half-way point, then quarters, then eighths. Now divide the number of stitches you need to pick up by 8, and pick these up evenly between the pins.

If there is a repeat or striped pattern in the knitting, it is easy to work out how many stitches to pick up between each repeat in the same way: divide the total number of stitches by the number of stripes/patterns, which will give the number of stitches to pick up in each repeat (see p93).

PICKING UP FROM THE SURFACE

Stitches can be picked up from the surface of the knitting for making pocket flaps, pleats, and any kind of decorative motif. The stitches on the surface of the knitting are probably more even and reliable than those at the edge. The number of stitches should be calculated in the same way as before, measuring across the area to be picked up, whether horizontally, vertically, or diagonally. Any part of the stitch can be picked up, ie sides of stitches, or the bars across the top.

With practice, it is almost possible to pick up the right number of stitches by feel, but it is vital to the look of the finished piece to get it right. There is nothing worse than a front band buckling with too many stitches, or pulling in with too few; so a quick calculation is invaluable.

HOW TO PICK THEM UP

The quickest and easiest action for picking up stitches is to use the right-hand needle only, like a crochet hook, and to lift and knit each stitch immediately onto the needle. If the yarn is held in the left hand (as in crochet), this movement is even quicker. The alternative is to pick up loops onto the needle first, then to knit them off, but this is more laborious.

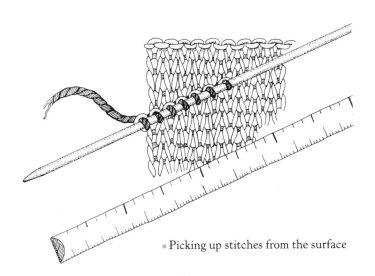

■ Picking up stitches from the surface

METHODS OF COLOUR KNITTING

The simplest way of producing a colourful effect in knitting is to use one colour at a time, in the form of stripes.

STRIPES

One could spend weeks experimenting and playing with arrangements of stripes; the variations in size, spacing, and proportions of stripes are limitless, and can give very different effects. Stripes can be any size, large or small, to the point where they are too wide or narrow to repeat or read as stripes. They could be wide bands of colour that almost envelope a garment, or stripes as narrow as two rows, or even one row (see p31, different types of needle for dealing with odd-row stripes). They can be regular, repeating stripes either in bold tonal contrast, or in soft, gentle colours; or they can be placed in rhythms of wide and narrow bands.

Narrow stripes will read as stripes from close up, but from a distance will merge into an all-over effect; eg narrow red and yellow stripes will appear as an orangey colour from a distance. Even the simplest form of pattern-making can be explored and pushed to its limits to see what effects can be achieved.

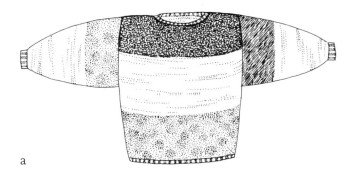

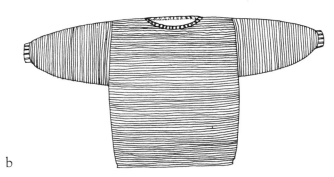

■ Stripes: a) wide bands of colour
    b) narrow stripes which merge into a texture

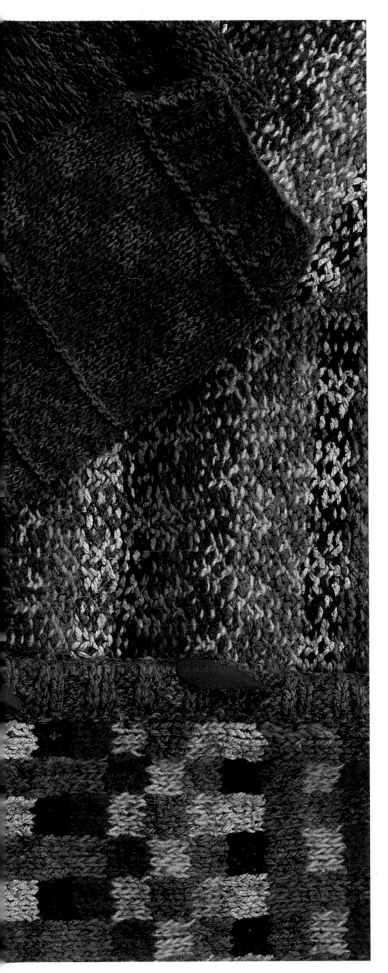

SLIP-STITCHES

If stripes do not appeal, or if you want to get away from a horizontal pattern-effect, there is a simple step you can take without things becoming technically complicated. Stripes do not necessarily have to read as horizontals, as stitches can be slipped to break up the line, and make completely different patterns and textures, while still only working with one colour at a time.

Characteristics: the character of a slipped-stitch fabric is similar to jacquard (see below) in that the yarn is stranded across the back where stitches are slipped (although usually only one or two stitches are slipped at a time); this tends to pull in the width very slightly.

However, it differs from the other colour methods in that slipped stitches also pull *up vertically*, making the growth of the knitting a little slower; and the fabric is altogether thicker than a non-slip-stitch fabric.

A wide variety of effects is possible in slip-stitch, but the overall effect is of small patterns and textures. For more striking, larger-scale patterns use jacquard or intarsia.

JACQUARD

Often called 'fairisle', this term means working with two or more colours in a row, knitting a few stitches in each colour, while the other(s) strands or weaves in at the back.

Characteristics: visually, jacquard is typified by multi-coloured patterns or repeating motifs. It is thick and warm to handle because two or more yarns are being used in each row. However, take care to knit with a good tension, or it can pull in widthways. Also, the yarn not being knitted should be woven in at the back to prevent long strands which will catch and pull.

The simplest way of knitting jacquard is to use only two colours in each row, although more can be used, making a thicker fabric. If a more varied colourful effect is wanted, use two in a row, with one or both changing every few rows. This tends to give a horizontal effect to the pattern, but with careful planning it need not be too dominant.

Jacquard knitting samples, showing weaving and stranding

Knitting Techniques

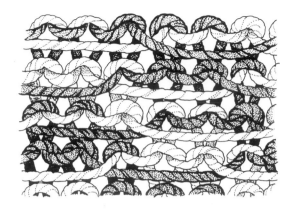
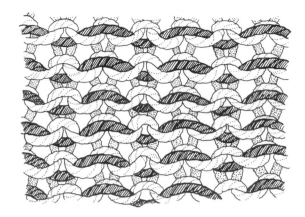

The reverse side of jacquard knitting showing
a) stranding, b) weaving-in

WEAVING IN USING BOTH HANDS

Begin by holding a yarn in each hand, over the forefingers, and once round the little fingers.
1 Knit row: a) right hand knitting, b) left hand knitting

a) RH knitting, LH weaving:

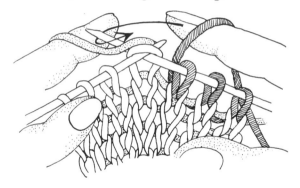

i) K st with RH, holding LH yarn **below**
ii) K next st with RH, holding LH yarn **above**

b) LH knitting, RH weaving:

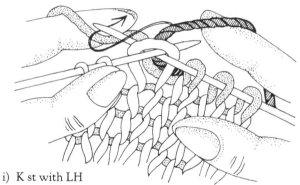

i) K st with LH
ii) needle in next st,
RH yarn over **as if** to knit, LH yarn over,
RH yarn **off**, and make st (say 'over, over, off, through')

2 Purl row: a) right hand purling, b) left hand purling

a) RH purling, LH weaving:

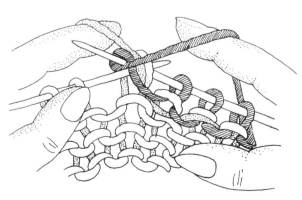

i) purl st with RH, holding LH yarn below
ii) P next st with RH, holding LH yarn above; rep i and ii

b) LH purling, RH weaving

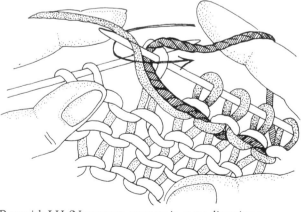

i) P st with LH (Note: yarn must go in same direction over
needle as it does in RH purling)
ii) needle in next st,
RH yarn **under** needle, LH yarn **over** needle, RH yarn
off, and make st (say 'under, over, off, through'); rep i and ii

WEAVING-IN AND STRANDING

With only two colours in a row, it is simple to weave in on the reverse of the knitting, either holding the colours on two different fingers in one hand, or one in each hand. People who have learnt knitting from childhood, perhaps at school, or who come from an area with a strong tradition of knitting, may well have learnt to weave in the yarns. For those who have not used the method before, it is worth taking a closer look at why it is done, and assessing the advantages and disadvantages:

- If the unknitted yarn is stranded, the stretch of the knitting will be limited by the straight strands of yarn across the back. If it is woven, it travels up and down in a waving motion rather than straight across, and so has more stretch.
- Stranding is fine over one or two stitches, but over more, long floats will be produced that can catch on the fingers and pull. Also, it is difficult to keep the stranded yarn evenly tensioned without pulling it too tight.
- If weaving is mastered, it is never necessary to drop a yarn and pick up another; both are held all the time, and so do not get tangled.
- One characteristic of weaving-in that might not be suitable for some designs is that the second yarn can show slightly on the front (depending on the type of yarn, and the needle size/yarn thickness used). This can have an attractive, softening effect, but if very clear, undiluted colours are wanted in the pattern, stranding might be preferable.
- To save darning in loose ends at colour changes, all ends can be woven in for a few stitches, and snipped off. This saves an enormous amount of work in a multi-coloured design, where otherwise all the ends would have to be sewn in afterwards.

If you are going to do much jacquard knitting and can see that weaving-in is going to be useful, then it is worth learning, even though it might need a lot of practice to achieve an even tension and speed. If you decide to use both hands, it will feel a bit like starting to knit all over again; but when mastered, it is almost as quick as knitting with one colour, and it is possible to knit without watching your hands. These instructions are for weaving the back (unused) colour on alternate sts, but longer strands could be left. The four stages are shown on the opposite page.

INTARSIA

When motifs or areas of colour are so large or far apart that it seems wasteful to carry the other yarn across, work with a separate ball for each colour, and let it travel only across its own area, twisting with its neighbouring colour at each join. Care is needed at the edge of each colour area so that the stitches don't become loose. Vertical joins are more difficult to control, and are easier in some yarns than others: cotton will show every unevenness, whereas fluffier yarns such as mohair help to conceal joins.

Intarsia is also useful for the occasional one or two stitches of a colour which occur in a vertical stripe, and the yarn can be carried up the fabric vertically, and knitted where necessary.

If there are a lot of different colours being used, it is easier to use short lengths of yarn, or to wind each yarn onto a small piece of card, rather than trying to cope with lots of heavy balls of wool.

Intarsia is the best way to get large, clear areas of colour without extra thickness, or tension problems.

- Intarsia: a) each area of colour has its own yarn
b) reverse of block pattern, holding each thread on a card

a

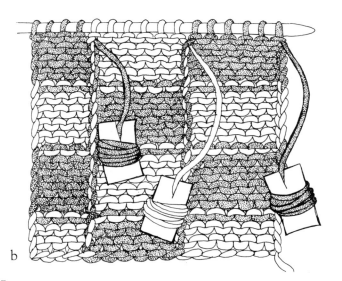

b

'Collage' jumper by Susan Duckworth, using the freedom of
intarsia to create a pattern in colour and texture

PLANNING THE BEST METHOD

Always try and use the method most suitable for your design: in other words, use whatever is easiest! The resulting fabric will be more successful if there have been no technical difficulties.

EXAMPLES

- A jumper with vertical stripes, or a coloured pattern with a vertical emphasis will be much easier to knit sideways across the body, than upwards while trying to manage lots of colours in each row in a vertical arrangement.
- If the design has a large motif or picture on the front and back, don't try knitting in the round in intarsia, as the yarns will be at the wrong end of each colour area next time round. If you particularly want to avoid seams

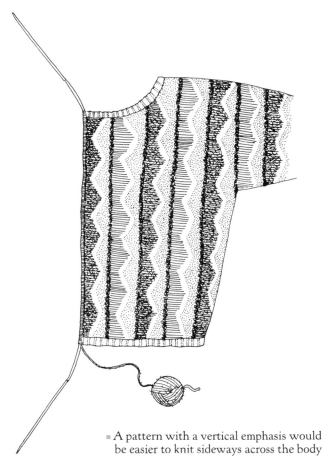

- A pattern with a vertical emphasis would be easier to knit sideways across the body

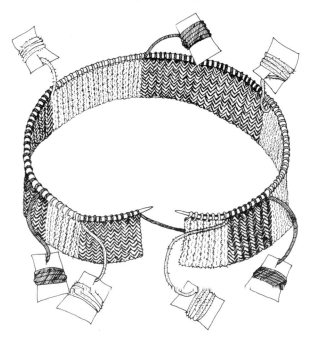

- Intarsia patterns cannot be knitted in the round, as the yarn will be left at the wrong end of each colour area

in this kind of design, try knitting sideways again, so that there is no shoulder seam; and then the side seams could be grafted.

- For a jacquard pattern, try and limit the colours to two in a row, to make it easier to knit.
- If the design has a diagonal effect, try increasing and decreasing to tilt the fabric so that you are still *knitting* horizontally, but producing bias or zig-zag knitting.
- If you find it awkward and cumbersome to use more than one colour at a time, see how many different effects you can achieve with a slip-stitch pattern.

4
TEXTURE

Texture in knitting is produced in the simplest way by turning the stitch from plain (knit-face) to purl on the surface of the fabric, so that either the smooth face of the knit stitch, or the raised bar of the purl stitch is presented. This can be used in different combinations, ie stocking stitch, reverse stocking stitch, moss stitch, garter stitch, or combinations of these stitches. For bolder effects you could experiment with crossing stitches over each other (cables and cross-over stitches) either singly or in groups; increasing and decreasing to form bobbles and embossed motifs; making holes (K2 tog, yarn over); or slipping stitches – all these give scope for textured patterns. Any combination of different stitches can be used and, once again, the possibilities in design are limitless.

PATTERNS IN TEXTURE

Textured stitches can be placed freely anywhere on the garment, in blocks or stripes, or in asymmetric, free-formed shapes. Using a good smooth yarn in a plain colour, it would be possible to forget about designing with colour, and concentrate solely on textured patterns, ranging from bold relief designs in cables, bobbles or embossed motifs to softer more subtle effects using knit, purl and moss stitch.

In order for a textured pattern to show clearly, an appropriate sort of yarn needs to be used, and it must be knitted at a fairly close tension. Textured or fancy yarns disguise the stitches, and the plainer and more firmly spun the yarn is, the more clearly the stitches will show.

In the past, textured stitches were used more than they are now, as fancy yarns and colours were not available to provide interest and pattern. One of the best surviving examples of traditional textured knitting can be seen in the fishermen's ganseys from the coastal villages of Britain, where the well-organised use of knit, purl and moss stitch shows clearly in rich patterning in the smooth, worsted-spun navy blue wool knitted in a firm, weather-proof tension (5-ply wool with 2¼mm (size 13) needles). The more ornate Aran sweaters from Ireland made use of bolder effects in cables and bobbles, usually in a natural unbleached white wool which showed the patterns beautifully.

Cotton will also show stitches clearly; in fact cotton always needs to be knitted with great care as any unevenness will show. Mercerised cotton is particularly clear and firm for knitting textured patterns. Cotton was used for knitting bedspreads in the 19th and early 20th centuries, and there are examples surviving which show a wealth of textured knitting patterns (see illustration).

RANDOM PATTERNING

Because it is possible to work so freely in handknitting, textured patterns need not always be organised in regular blocks or repeats – motifs can be placed anywhere at will. Cables need not lie in tidy columns, but can travel randomly over a garment. The only thing to remember in free patterning is that different types of stitch will pull in or push out the fabric, creating unevennesses. The design may therefore have to be planned in such a way that none of its parts are stretched or pulled, which would make the result appear unintentional: the overall effect must look deliberate to be successful, however free the patterning is.

EMBOSSED PATTERNS

Knitting by hand also gives the freedom to knit only part of a row or to work on a small group of stitches at a time, so it is possible to knit embossed motifs, pleats, bulges (eg constructed like sock heels) or frills, in patterns that are built out in relief, making the richly textured surface almost three-dimensional.

This is taken a stage further when motifs are added after the main fabric has been knitted, picking up stitches from the surface and knitting pieces that grow out from the fabric (see chapter 3 p41). Stitches can be picked up in any direction and at any angle, knitted to any size, and knitted or sewn back in, breaking away completely from the horizontal nature of knitted rows.

An early 20th-century cotton bedspread from the author's collection, knitted in diagonal squares with a traditional textured pattern of leaves and ridges, joined in groups of four squares so that the 'leaves' come together

Mixing colour in knitting by using textured stitches and jacquard patterns

LACE KNITTING

A finer texture in knitting is produced by knitted lace stitches, where the pattern is created by knitting holes and decreases in formation. Lace patterns do not have to be worked conventionally in delicate yarns and a fine tension, but are very effective in heavier yarns, making strong patterns of holes on a thicker background. The patterns show up best if the tension is kept fairly firm, not too open or floppy, as the holes will then contrast more strongly with the background. If early pieces of lace knitting are examined (for instance Shetland shawls, or Victorian cotton knitted lace), although they may at first appear quite open with large-scale holes, closer inspection of the areas of plain stocking stitch will illustrate the fineness of the needle gauge (see illustration p10).

MIXING COLOUR

Textured stitches can be put to uses other than simply creating textures and patterns. If certain stitches are combined with coloured patterns, even in the simplest arrangement of stripes, the colours will mix in unexpected ways; for example, a 2-row stripe pattern worked in stocking stitch shows clearly, whereas if it is worked in moss stitch (K1,P1) the colours will be blurred and mixed by the purl stitches to give a blended all-over colour with a faint stripe (see Stitch Library sample 2).

More pronounced textures such as bobbles, bramble stitch, cross-over, woven or cable stitches, will also help to disguise stripes and mix up colours, resulting in rich and varied fabrics. Sometimes the colour-change can emphasise the texture of the stitch, for instance in a cable where a horizontal stripe jumps from a purl background to the twisted cable, accenting the relief texture.

Another dramatic way to make stripes more interesting is to use increases and decreases, placed regularly throughout the row, as in some lace stitches (Stitch Library 31–35). This has the effect of moving the stripes up and down into zigzag waves; and can be made more textural by introducing purl-face stitches as well.

Perhaps the most useful of all textured stitches for colour-mixing are slip-stitches (see p43, and Stitch Library 2d, 3 & 4); even when working with only one colour at a time in stripes, textures and small repeat patterns can be made by slipping certain stitches which are then stretched vertically across the rows, so breaking up the horizontal stripes completely. It is possible to produce small repeat patterns almost like jacquard, but with more texture.

TEXTURE FOR WARMTH

Not only do different textured stitches affect the look of the surface of the knitted fabric; they will also alter the thickness, the weight, the amount of stretch, and the drape.

In the past, texture was used to provide warmth, and textured patterns were mainly used for extra weather-proofing on the chest and back of guernsey sweaters, in the same way as the patterned yokes of Scandinavian garments provided vital warmth by the extra yarn in coloured jacquard patterns.

The thickness of a knitted pattern is caused by stitches being pushed out from the surface: by crossing them over each other, as in cabling and cross-over stitches; or by slipping stitches, where they are pulled up across the rows to make a thicker fabric. Embossed motifs also give extra thickness in the form of relief motifs, leaves, bobbles or ruching. With the extra depth caused by the crossing-over of stitches or relief motifs, the width of the knitting is pulled in to create greater thickness, therefore more stitches and more yarn are used. In slip-stitches the length is also pulled up so that the knitting grows more slowly, as it is creating depth as well as length. In other words, heavily textured knitting is necessarily slower to produce, and uses more yarn than plainer patterns.

TEXTURE FOR COOL FABRICS

Similarly, textured stitches can be employed to make a cooler fabric. Lace stitches use holes to form patterns, and here again they can be used in regular all-over patterns, grouped in areas, or used at random.

The hole as a unit is made by 'O (yarn over) and K2tog', or 'S1, K1, psso, O', or simply a 'yarn over', which makes an extra stitch. This can be used as a single motif placed anywhere, or in formation as in traditional lace stitches. The slant of the decrease needs to be planned, as it changes the look of the pattern. (The stitches slant to the right in 'K2 tog', and to the left in 'S1, K1, psso'.) In most lace stitches, the 'O' is still balanced by a decrease (so that the number of stitches stays constant), but the two do not necessarily come next to each other, as can be seen in the Stitch Library, samples 31, 34 and 35. This has the effect, mentioned earlier, of making the stitches slant away from the increase towards the decrease, and results in a more textured, wavy surface.

Amongst other open-work stitches for cooler fabrics is ladder stitch, where vertical open-work sections are made by dropping stitches in a controlled way, letting them run to the bottom of the knitting. This can be very effective alongside a cable, contrasting well with twisted cable stitches; or stitches can be dropped a little way, then stretched back up over the ladder (ie butterfly stitch).

Horizontal open areas are made by inserting rows of elongated stitches, either by using a much larger needle for a single row, or perhaps more easily by wrapping the yarn two or three times round the needle for each stitch, knitting one loop only in the following row.

TEXTURED STITCHES
FOR SHAPING GARMENTS

If textured stitches are compared in a sample with stocking stitch, using the same number of stitches and rows, it can be seen clearly how much the fabric is pulled in or up: see the samples in chapter 3. It is a challenge in designing knitting to use this effect in the shaping of garments, rather than tailoring the shape by increasing and decreasing. In this way the structure can be kept absolutely simple, working in squares or rectangles, and all shaping can be done by the inventive use of different stitches. The most obvious example is the use of ribbing to gather in cuffs and welts, but this can be extended to fitting waists with cable or any cross-over or other stretchy stitch; cuffs can also be knitted in twice-knit stitch, or any stitch that pulls in dramatically. For more fullness in sleeves, moss stitch could be used to spread the stitches more widely, contrasted with a firm or stretchy-stitched edging (see chapter 7).

Textured stitches can also be used in narrow contrasting bands or stripes to pull in or push out the tension, making a knitted fabric like seersucker.

Greek socks and armbands knitted without seams in very hardwearing, highly-spun yarn

53

5
COLOUR

The process of choosing colours for a design is something that everyone has to work out for themselves, as the appeal of colour varies so much individually. Also, different colours and colour combinations affect people in different ways, and where a group of colours may strike one person as memorable, significant, or beautiful, it may not another. However, there are stages of looking, noticing and being aware that can be learnt so that it becomes a habit to notice and analyse colours; it is possible to train your eye to select colours with greater discrimination, and this will help the process of choosing those that will work well together in designs.

The first step is to be aware of colours in our surroundings: often we do not consciously notice colours, but a mood may be lightened by particular colours without us realising why – woods in autumn, or a bright flowerbed which may suddenly make our spirits lift. So firstly we must appreciate this when it happens, and pause, look and take note.

The second step is to analyse why these particular colours have caught our attention. We might think we have noticed only one or two, but often it is a matter of combined effect, where the colours in the surroundings or background have made that particular colour stand out.

The quality of a colour depends also on the nature of the materials; for instance the richness of old Mediterranean roof tiles would not be the same if they were made of synthetic materials. Why not? Because the colour would be more uniform, less varied than it is in the fired clay, which has many shades of terracotta and warm browns caused by the firing process and by the way it has weathered. Moreover these same roofs will seem richer and brighter according to the colour of the sky they are seen against: if the sky is blue, the roofs will glow more orange, the background reacting against the colour, making it appear stronger.

The proportions of a group of colours can be vital to the way they work together. A group of yellow, grey, and pink could be bright and dazzling, but if the grey were formed of areas of varying greys, with only a little yellow and a dash of pink, it could give a cool effect with small jewels of colour. So this is something else to consider

when a group of colours has caught your eye: try and notice *how much* of each colour there is, and if the brightest or most significant colour covers the largest area, or whether there is only a small amount.

Although our tastes in colour vary, there are circumstances where colours come together naturally in a way that is generally accepted as beautiful: for instance, the colours in a sky at sunset, when the colours blend into each other and are changing constantly; or perhaps the colour of bluebells in a wood in spring. If you try and find a knitting yarn to match the blue of these flowers, you very soon discover that they contain several shades of blue and purple; and that the dim light in the wood, the dark browns of the trees, and the fresh green of young leaves provide a setting for the blues which gives them a luminosity they would not have if seen against a different background, such as an open hillside, or if the same blues were painted onto white paper. So often in the colours we see around us there is more to each colour than meets the eye: so that a rich brown may contain several shades of brown, from grey-brown to red-brown; or a stone wall contain tones of grey that are richly varied from purple to blue or green-grey, giving an overall effect of a colour – grey – which is in fact built of a multitude of different shades only apparent close up.

The ability to work with colour comes more easily to some people than to others, but it can be trained and developed once we increase our awareness of the colours around us, and by constant questioning, memorising and note-taking.

Colour theory provides basic rules about primary, secondary and complementary colours, and will help us to understand and analyse why particular colours react to each other in a certain way.

The complementary colour to each primary is composed of the other two primary colours, red being complementary to green, which = blue + yellow, which therefore bears no relation to red, being as different from red within the spectrum as it can be. The colours we see in our surroundings are usually softer and more blended than pure primaries and secondaries, but there can still be a strong visual reaction when, for example, shades of red and green are placed together. So in order to appreciate subtlety and variations beyond carefully calculated shades, we must learn to observe, absorb, and eventually translate the essence of what we have seen into our designs.

Working from source material: yarns, wool windings, and knitted samples for colour and texture

55

The third step is to record what we see; we might ask: Why is that colour so bright? What is it seen against? Record with paints or crayons on the spot if possible, or even jot down written notes about colours you have seen, for example 'small amount primrose yellow, next to large area in various greys, with touch of purple'. Then go home and find yarns, or paints or crayons, or tear paper from magazines to use as collage and so make 'coloured' notes.

Another way of helping to develop an awareness of colour is to collect postcards, or compile a scrapbook from magazine photos, reproductions of paintings, landscapes, groups of buildings, or whatever has a quality of colour that you would like to remember. Gradually you will find that colours will jump out at you wherever you are, and you will be aware of all sorts of subtleties of colour that you had not noticed before.

Lastly, a combination of colours has to be chosen and translated into yarns for a knitted design. If you are working from something you have seen, this will be a guide; but it is a big leap from seeing colour in a picture or landscape and knitting a pattern in coloured yarns.

It is often a mistake to try to reproduce in knitting exactly what you have seen. To knit a landscape or reproduce a picture in knitting requires a huge amount of skill as well as artistic ability, and can easily end in disappointment if there are technical problems, or the yarns do not give the effect you want. You need to decide what quality it is that you want to translate into knitting: whether it is the colours, textures, pattern; a general hazy, misty effect; or bright dots and stripes. Although extracting and simplifying is a difficult process, the results are usually more convincing and appropriate to the technique.

So the next step is to arrive at a chosen group of yarns. Sometimes, when you think your colours would make a good, interesting, rich combination, you might find that as balls of wool on a table they look disappointingly dull. At this point you may decide to leave your original inspiration behind, and make your group of colours work on their own.

As well as considering the proportions of each colour, the tonal values are also important, and sometimes a touch of something very dark or very light can bring a group of colours to life. Another trick is to add a touch of a complementary colour. It need not be a 'pure' complementary, but perhaps a softer version: ie if working in a range of blues, or blue/greys, a touch of orange may be added – and the shade of orange is important, too; it will make a great difference to the group if a warm orange or a cooler orange is used, and you may need to veer more towards yellow, or red, or even a rusty terracotta, depending on whether the blues are cold or warm. This is where personal judgement comes in: and don't be afraid to experiment!

BUILDING COLOUR

One of the most exciting ways of using colour in knitting, as in weaving, is to build a colour out of units of varying shades to produce a rich, vibrant effect. If you look at landscapes, or photos of fields or towns, there may be areas of green or brown or red. Look more closely, and you will notice that these are built up of different shades of each colour – roof tiles of varying tones, woodland composed of different types of trees and leaves – producing a general colour formed of tiny units of different shades, like a mosaic. Although a continuous yarn is used in knitting, the fabric is built of units of the stitch, which can be used like brush strokes in an Impressionist painting to build up a strong overall colour, which on closer inspection reveals different shades, giving extra intensity and interest.

Why are Persian carpets or kelim rugs so rich in their colouring, and often more interesting than machine-made copies? It might be that the dye lots have changed slightly throughout the piece, giving a more vibrant and varied colour that holds the eye and keeps the interest far more readily than would a plain uniform colour.

It is a great challenge to knit something that is striking from a distance, but becomes more interesting and varied when looked at closely. This could be achieved by working with different shades of, say, green (blue-greens, yellow-greens) for different stitches in each row: ie knitting jacquard with two or more colours in a small geometric pattern. It could also be done by working in narrow (1- or 2-row) stripes of each shade; or by breaking up the stripes with a slip-stitch (see chapter 3 p43) to give an overall rich effect of green, which on closer inspection is seen to contain different shades.

WOOL WINDINGS

If you are working from a group of colours chosen from something you have seen, and have noted down the colours on paper, and found the yarn which seems to suggest the right shades and depths of colour, you will then need to know how they are going to look when knitted up. A halfway step is to wind the wool onto card in stripes of the shades chosen, trying to get the proportions right. This gives the solid yarn effect that you would get in a knitted fabric, but is much quicker than knitting a sample, and it is easy to alter colours and proportions if you are not satisfied.

You will need pieces of card of postcard stiffness or thicker (any old cardboard packets will do) cut into strips, at least 5 × 10cm; and sticky-tape, preferably double-sided. Stick a piece of the double-sided sticky-tape along the back of the card, and begin winding the yarn around it, keeping it touching edge to edge to cover the card completely. Change colour when appropriate for the effect you want, and the tape will hold the ends firm.

These wool-windings will give a much more accurate impression of the density of coloured yarn in knitting than can be achieved with paint or crayon on paper.

DYEING

If you are working in the way that has been described, using outside source material for inspiration to help choose the colours for your designs, you will need to collect a wide range of coloured yarns to give you the subtle permutations necessary to work from what you have seen. This takes time, but need not be expensive if you get into the habit of picking up odd balls whenever you see yarns for sale. And dyeing your own yarn means you can design your own colours and thereby enlarge your range even further. It is fun to do, and can be carried out with very little equipment.

Wool is the easiest fibre to dye as it takes colour readily. Silk can be dyed with the same kind of dye as wool, but the colour is not absorbed so easily, so dark shades are more difficult. Cotton and linen need different types of dye, as do synthetics; but if you want to try dyeing on a small scale, there is a comprehensive dye available in small packs from hardware shops and haberdashers that can be used on mixed fibres, either in cold water, or by the boiling method.

NATURAL DYES

Dyes from natural sources work well on wool and silk. The range of colours possible from plant material is beautiful, using wild plants that you find (check first that you are not over-picking any varieties that are scarce), or dried plant material that can be bought from suppliers. Information can be obtained from local Guilds of Weavers, Spinners and Dyers, or similar groups (see List of Suppliers). Natural dyes have a reputation for giving soft, subdued colours, but strong shades can also be obtained, particularly when using plants grown in warm climates. Look at paintings and portraits from the past for evidence of the richness of colour achieved in yarn and clothing before chemical dyes were invented: rich golds, madder and cochineal reds, indigo blues, and greens in the costumes in Italian frescos, Elizabethan green velvets, and Gainsborough's pale blue silk dresses.

CHEMICAL DYES

Chemical dyes for wool and silk are also readily available, in very easy-to-use kit form, supplied in solution in plastic bottles in a basic kit of red, blue, yellow and black, from which endless combinations and shades are possible.

The two main differences between natural and chemical dyes are that in natural dyes, shades are less predictable and the process takes longer, as the yarn needs to be prepared first using a mordant. This enables it to react with the dye and absorb the colour, and different mordants result in different colours from the same dye. The dyeing process itself cannot be hurried, and needs to be an all-day event. There is a residue of plant material to get rid of afterwards (good compost?), and occasional weird smells from the mordants and dye materials – all of which add to the mystery and fun in experimenting with plant dyes.

Chemical dyes are fast to light and washing, and straightforward to use: it is easy to repeat colours if measurements are recorded carefully, and the whole process can take little over an hour – although again, dyeing is rather like baking bread, more successful if not hurried.

Natural dyes are more mysterious and less predictable; more of a challenge for the adventurous, and of course cheaper if you are collecting your own dye plants.

EQUIPMENT

For any kind of dyeing, you will need the following: a skein winder – yarn needs to be dyed in skeins so that the dye can penetrate evenly; fine cotton or wool for tying the skeins to prevent tangling; a wool winder, for winding the skeins into balls for knitting; pans for boiling the yarn (not the same ones that are used for cooking); a cooker, or gas or electric hob – or if you are going to work with larger quantities of yarn (eg a kilo at a time), a Burco (or similar) electric boiler is ideal. Plastic buckets are useful for soaking and rinsing; and lastly, space for hanging yarns to dry. Ideally dyeing should be done on a sunny day so that yarn can be hung out-of-doors, making less of an intrusion in the home.

ADVANTAGES

The main advantage of dyeing your own yarn is the enormous choice of colours made available: the variety of shades obtainable is endless. Using natural dyes, differently mordanted yarns can be put in the same dyebath to achieve miraculously different shades: for instance, the colours obtained from the weld plant range from a strong bright yellow to a dull khaki brown, depending on the mordant used; similarly the reds from madder and cochineal can result in very bright colour right through to dull browns and purples.

Page 58–9
■ Basic dyeing equipment: scales, pans, electric hob, measuring jug, notebook, rubber gloves, dye kit (dyes, beakers and syringes for measuring).
Inset Tie-dyed and space-dyed wool: the top skein is still partly tied; the balls of wool have small areas of colour from dip-dyeing; the bottom skein shows pattern from single ties

Colour

It might sound a time-consuming process, particularly as the knitting itself takes long enough! But dyeing is like baking: there is preparation time, then periods of waiting and occasional stirring when other work can be done, or samples knitted.

Dyeing several shades at once obviously saves time as well, and this can also be done by putting different coloured wools into one dyebath. Natural shades of wool from white to dark grey can be dyed as light, medium or darker tones of a colour.

DYEING PROCESS

1 If the yarn is not already in a skein, wind it onto a skein-winder (failing this, round a chair back, or similar), tying the first end firmly onto the winder so that it can be found again. Twist the two ends round each other, then tie them round the thickness of the skein (see photograph).

   Using short lengths of soft string or spare yarn, tie in three places round the skein, loosely in a figure-of-eight; this helps prevent tangling.

2 Weigh the yarn, and make a note of it.

3 If the yarn is still oily (ie straight from the spinner or mill), scour by filling a sink or bucket with very hot water containing a little detergent, and holding on to the string used for tying, plunge the yarn gently in and out of the water. Squeeze gently, and rinse in several changes of clean hot water.

   If it has already been scoured, or is obviously clean, soak gently in cold water with a few drops of detergent.

4 Make up the dye pot or mordant, according to your recipe.

5 Immerse the yarn, turning gently while heating slowly. Most dyes need to be brought to boiling point over about one hour, but follow recipe.

6 Boil according to recipe. Some dyes take more strongly if the skein is left to cool in the liquid.

7 Rinse thoroughly in clean water which should be at the same temperature as the yarn when you take it out. NOTE: *Felting* is caused by washing in sudden changes of temperature, with a lot of agitation (and soap): so treat the yarn very gently to *avoid* tangling and felting.

8 When the water rinses clear, squeeze gently, and hang to drip-dry. If the yarn is very springy, it will help to dry it under slight tension.

SPACE-DYEING

A further step in designing your own coloured yarns is to control the dyeing process to produce a space-dyed yarn; this will give extra pattern in the knitting. Either dip the skein partly into the dye to give patches of colour (the undyed part could be left natural, or dyed a different shade later); or tie the skein tightly at intervals – this prevents the dye penetrating and you are left with spots, flecks or patches of the original colour at intervals on the yarn.

Space- or tie-dyed yarn can be used to great effect in knitting, producing a random element which could be knitted in stripes, blocks, free areas of intarsia, or in a geometric pattern, contrasting with plain-dyed yarn.

It can be planned and controlled, as in woven 'ikat' fabrics, but this is more difficult than in weaving where the threads appear on the cloth in much the same position as when tied to go on the loom. The amount the yarn is taken up in knitting is hard to calculate, and will vary according to the tension and type of stitch used, and change according to the width of the knitted fabric. However, there are some fine examples of Andean knitting with patterns formed by space-dyed yarn on hats, where it would be easier to control than on a larger garment (see Bibliography).

6
PATTERN

Where do we begin in making patterns? Where do we find inspiration and how do we apply it to designing knitting? As with colour, we are surrounded by pattern in all sorts of forms and it is a question of knowing where and how to look, record, and translate what we see into a suitable design for knitting.

Some patterns stand out and are easy to visualise: brickwork on buildings, striped fences, formal flowerbeds; also displays of goods set out in rows in shops, or fruit and vegetables on market stalls, which suggest shapes and textures easily knitted as patterns in rows. Sometimes larger scale patterns are not immediately obvious, but may be glimpsed occasionally: avenues of trees, patterns of fields on a hillside, or aerial photographs which reveal patterns such as houses placed along a road, with rows of gardens behind.

Alternatively, it may be a more elusive kind of pattern such as the swirls and eddies of a stream, or the contrasting foliage of trees in a wood. Sometimes in crowds or groups of people such as dancers, one is aware of patterns made by the group moving in formation, making constantly-changing shapes and rhythms.

Once again you need to make a mental note of what you have seen, and then record notes on paper in some way. The act of drawing or sketching helps to clarify what it is you want to remember – because you have to start extracting and simplifying immediately.

How does one define what pattern is? It does not have to be regular or symmetrical, but it always has a rhythm and a certain repetitiveness, either through the repeat of a motif, a grid of stripes or checks, or the swirl or curve of a line.

An easy way to begin a search for ideas for patterns is to look at photographs in books or magazines. Someone

Working from a photograph, simplifying first into stripes of texture and pattern, and then working a stylised jacquard pattern of circles containing different textures

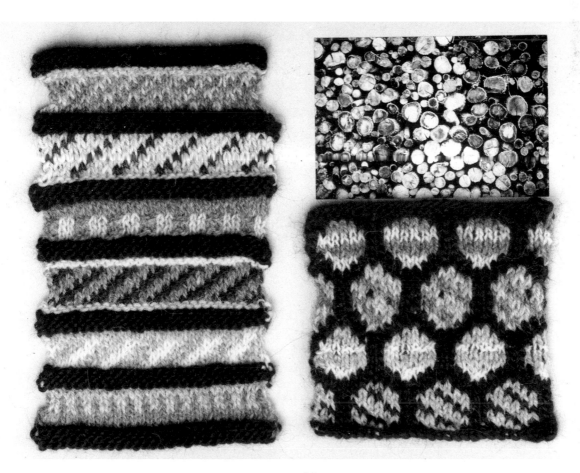

■ A landscape with areas of striped patterning

examples of these, as well as artefacts, from jewellery to wrought iron, pottery and textiles, often exquisitely patterned. A few hours spent looking round a museum or art gallery should leave one feeling inspired by pattern and colour, and impatient to start designing.

Once you reach the stage of absorbing and noting down ideas, then those ideas will need to be simplified and adjusted to fit the technique of knitting; or the technique adapted to achieve the desired effect.

STRIPES

■

To begin at the beginning in the simplest way, why not let the technique dictate the pattern: knitting is performed horizontally in rows, and is therefore ideally suited to striped patterning. Stripes form one of the boldest kinds of pattern there is; they occur in the natural world in animals and plants, and have been used by man in all sorts of decoration since primitive times, from body painting to pottery, baskets, and woven blankets.

As stripes are composed of lines repeated in a regular or irregular rhythm, it is worth looking first at the kind of lines that can be produced in knitting. The character of a line is dictated by the technique and materials used: for instance a line drawn in charcoal on paper has a different character from a pencil line, or of a woven line. Looking down from a hilltop, the line of a road is different in character from that of a footpath made by people treading and wearing the ground from one place to another. Knitting makes lines which have their own quality, varying according to the yarn and stitch used, from smooth to fluffy, or textured. A full appreciation of the different characteristics of the lines that can be made in knitting means there is a wider field of reference for designing with more interest, subtlety or boldness.

As a starting point to designing a pattern of stripes, work from something seen – perhaps shadows, railings, or a ploughed field – and adjust and extract from what you have seen so that some of its character can be reflected in the knitting. Do you see the pattern as having stripes on a background, or are all the bands equally dominant? Is there a regular rhythm, or are the stripes grouped? Using more than two colours alters the balance, making a bigger repeat, and often a greater illusion of depth, with some stripes coming to the fore and other colours sinking back.

As discussed earlier (chapter 3 p41) stripes can look very different according to the scale, the width and the rhythm of the repeat. In knitting, colour and texture can be incorporated in an endless variety of combinations, using relief or textured stripes to emphasise or echo

else has already made a start here, by isolating a scene and selecting something which has caught their eye. Books of aerial photography, landscape, or townscape, are all rich in source material for pattern-making; as are nature books, with details of bird or animal markings, or plant and garden books. From this beginning, you will become aware of natural patterns occurring around you, and can begin to make notes of what you see, so as to make your own selections and interpretations.

As well as natural patterning, and patterns in our environment that have been caused, even unintentionally, by man, we are also surrounded by man-made patterns relative to other materials, such as walls, windows, stained glass, china and fabrics, to name only a few. In fact the choice is so vast that it is easy to become dazzled and to try, too soon, to apply a pattern we have seen directly to a design for knitting. The danger in this is to be too complicated, to try to include too much; besides which a pattern seen in another medium may not necessarily be appropriate to the technique or materials of knitting, or to making a garment or fabric design.

However, it will help us to develop an awareness of pattern, spacing and colour if we look at other sources, for example the decorative arts, such as Indian miniature paintings which are rich in the use of pattern. A museum such as the Victoria and Albert in London has many

■

Woolwinding proportions and colours taken from the landscape photograph above are shown top left. Samples are then knitted of patterns from different areas of the photograph, simplifying each area into a regular striped pattern, using different stitches to represent the textures of the landscape

coloured stripes. Look also at woven textiles in books or exhibitions: for instance woven rugs, North American Indian blankets, or Regency silks; see how bold and strong a striped design can be, or how it can be softened to a subtle effect in fine lines and pale shades.

Tonal contrasts could be experimented with, using dark shades of black (blue-black, greeny-black) with white, cream, or pale colours. Then progress to colour contrasts, using dazzling complementary colours; and see how it alters a pattern of stripes to change from black and white to red and green. Perhaps also experiment with the subtlety of white on white (or off-white): ie two different yarns such as creamy tussah silk and white wool; pure white cotton with a soft, unbleached white; or the shadow of a textured stripe in a white or natural shade.

It may seem an unambitious beginning to design something as straightforward as stripes; but a striped design takes on another character when used as a garment, bedspread or throw, emphasising the shape the fabric is covering.

DIAGONALS

Diagonal stripes follow the knitting technique comfortably, as in weaving where diagonals are also often used. Weaving is structured on a grid of vertical and horizontal threads, and similarly in knitting we work in horizontal rows: the stitches link together in vertical columns, and to step the colour or textured stitch to the right or left in every, or every alternate row, is a happy progression for a knitted pattern. Again, the character of the line can be varied, with textured stitches used in combination with colour: add a purl stitch to a stocking stitch coloured diagonal, and the line is softened and made less clear (see Stitch Library samples 25-28).

Stripes lead the eye, and can be used in areas to emphasise a certain direction. Diagonals can also be arranged in large-scale chevron or zig-zag patterns, and directed to meet at a centre point on a garment: this can make a flattering design (see p72).

A line or stripe of a single stitch has a different character of line when worked in horizontal, diagonal or vertical stripes. Vertically, a one-stitch stripe gives a smooth, clean line, as the shape of the stitch is smooth at the sides; and it shows more strongly as a vertical, because the knitted stitch is wider than it is tall. As a horizontal stripe, one row gives a very fine line, with the slightly zig-zag character that comes from the V-shape of the stitch. This can be broken into a subtle faintly-textured stripe by purling on a knit ground for the one row, which breaks up the colour continuity (Stitch Library sample 18). Diagonally, again a more broken line is made by the pointed corners of the V; for a more definite diagonal, at least two stitches are needed.

Don't be afraid to experiment.

Knitted grid and check patterns

VERTICALS

Vertical stripes work well in textured stitches such as rib, moss stitch stripes, cables, lace patterns, stripes of bobbles or embossed motifs. Coloured verticals are more difficult as they involve working with more than one yarn at a time, and a vertical colour join is sometimes difficult to perform neatly, as there is a weakness where the colour changes (see p45). This is disguised in diagonal stripes because the join does not always come in the same place. In spite of this, a vertical two-colour rib makes an acceptably bold edging, but it would take a very even knitter to sustain it satisfactorily over a longer length. The easier way to achieve coloured stripes in a vertical arrangement is to knit 'sideways' or across a garment so that although knitted horizontally, the stripes fall vertically (see p47).

GRIDS AND CHECKS

An obvious progression from stripes is to make check or grid patterns by crossing one sort of stripe with another, ie horizontal with vertical or diagonal. Try combining horizontal texture stripes with diagonal coloured stripes, or vice versa, and notice what other effects and shapes appear. An easy and effective composition is to combine vertical textures with horizontal colours, which can give added effects where the lines cross – the textured stitch may make the coloured stripe thicker, or kink it in some way. This makes an extra point of interest, where the technique of knitting takes over and makes its own contribution to the design.

Look at the various grids and check patterns around you for ideas to make your designs more interesting: wire netting, fences, windows and window panes. Notice what happens when the lines cross each other: is there any hesitation or thickness in the line at this point? In knitting, the cross-over points could be emphasised in various ways – with an added textured stitch or two, or dot of colour: a bobble, or a couple of purl stitches on a knit ground.

Trellis patterns are another kind of grid, composed of diagonals crossing, and so fall comfortably into a knitted pattern.

DOTS AND REPEAT MOTIFS

Small repeat motifs also suit the technique of knitting well, either in textured stitches, or jacquard coloured patterns. They can be positioned on a square grid, or in a trellis formation or half-drop pattern.

It is tempting to think only of colour when planning patterns, as designing with colour is so exciting and immediately rewarding; but used in an appropriate yarn, textured stitches can work well for repeat patterns. They can also be used to emphasise colour patterns, or to complement or echo colours: a motif could use purl stitches in the middle, giving a raised effect that brings the motif into relief; or a coloured motif might be echoed by using a textured stitch in the spaces between.

The pattern does not need to be a mechanical repeat in handknitting. Obviously it is easier to knit a regular design, to get into a rhythm of '5 blue, 2 red', or whatever, all the way along the row; nonetheless, we have the freedom when knitting by hand to bring in random changes which will give added interest in a spontaneous way – this is one of the special characteristics of working by hand. The occasional spot of another colour, or a motif of a different shape can easily be introduced, punctuating the rhythm of the design. At first glance it is a regular pattern, but there is something that holds the eye, and as you look more closely the variation within the pattern will become apparent.

GEOMETRIC

The dictionary defines geometric as 'patterns made from simple geometric forms, ie circles, rectangles, triangles, etc'. In knitting, circles are not as easy to accomplish as the other forms; but squares, triangles, zig-zags, diamonds and star patterns all knit well with infinite possible combinations; and geometric patterns work well in plain/purl textured stitches, or coloured patterns.

Look at books illustrating traditional fairisle knitting, or Scandinavian or Andean designs – geometric patterns lend themselves to colour knitting in all-over patterns, bands or borders – and they are very satisfying to knit, too, as they fall into a regular rhythm. And even though geometric patterns have been used so widely in traditional knitting, weaving and embroidery, there is always scope for individual interpretation. Traditionally, we

think of fairisle colours as gentle rather than startling, although they were sometimes rich, with surprisingly strong reds and golds. But choosing the colours yourself for even a simple geometric design immediately gives it an individual character.

If you dye your own colours, try using a space-dyed yarn in a geometric pattern to create a random effect within the regularity of the pattern. Or experiment with geometric designs in simple black and white combinations, perhaps using varying shades of blacks and off-blacks, whites and off-whites, for more interest. Perhaps even forget 'colour' and experiment with only white and off-white, or shiny yarns with duller or textured fibres: imagine a clear geometric pattern knitted in white silk and cream wool – it could be very effective.

MOTIFS

Motifs do not have to be used in repeat, but can be spaced at random, or used as individual decorative features. In this case the technique changes, as a motif in isolation will not want its colours carried across the main fabric; it should therefore be worked in intarsia or a combination of intarsia/jacquard.

There are a few technical points to consider here: firstly, a coloured motif on a plain ground will, if several colours are being used, make a thicker fabric at this point, so great care has to be taken both in the choice of yarn and in the knitting of it, so that the edges or outline are strong and the motif not too heavy in thickness for the background. The main fabric has to be firmly knitted in a good yarn, too, so that the coloured motifs do not stretch or pull it.

The visual effect must be planned so that the motifs balance, and the spacing looks right on the garment. Look at contemporary designers' work to see how they have dealt with spacing, balance and the knitting of motifs.

PICTORIAL/FLORAL

This leads on to more ornate patterning, which might cover the whole garment or fabric and allows for more flowing, broader effects than those achieved in motifs or geometric patterns.

An early example of richly patterned knitting – although all in one colour and using only purl stitches on a knit ground – is an early Dutch piece in the Victoria and Albert Museum, London. The forms here are quite complicated, incorporating wandering foliage with ornate leaf forms, and exotic animals and birds (see Bibliography). This amount of detail can only have been possible because it was knitted on such a fine scale; if it had been made in thicker yarn and needles, the figures would have been enormous. However, the piece illustrates the possibilities in knitting curves, which on this scale work well, although they are slightly stilted in the character typical of knitting.

Curved lines and shapes are always going to be more difficult in knitting than, say, embroidery, because of the grid-structure of knitting mentioned earlier, so that a curve is necessarily constructed of steps, as in computer graphics; and curved lines will therefore appear smoother on a smaller scale. The best curves in knitting occur when the stitches themselves are pulled or stretched across or round each other, ie in some lace patterns, where the holes and the increases and decreases distort the stitches

Repeat patterns: dots, stripes and geometric

into beautifully smooth curves and leaf shapes (see Stitch Library, samples 34 and 35). This is also true in cabling, where gradual or steeper curves are made by one or more stitches being crossed over others in snake-like forms which can be taken in any direction. It would be interesting to try using some of these types of stitches combined with colour to achieve successfully curving coloured forms.

Designing floral, figurative or pictorial patterns obviously involves considerably more draughtsmanship and artistry than a simple geometric pattern that follows the knitted stitch so comfortably. Whether the design is of flowers, trees, a landscape, a building, animals or birds, the shapes have at some point to be drawn, and then knitted, convincingly. Every line is important: the curve of a stem, the placing of fields, hedges, or whatever it might be; and not only does it have to be skilfully drawn, it then has to be satisfactorily transferred to the grid of the knitted structure. William Morris was a master at translating what he had seen in nature into fabric designs, capturing an 'intense feeling for nature...so different from the imitation of nature.. [of other designers' work]' (Niklaus Pevsner, *Pioneers of Modern Design*).

It might be tempting to knit a landscape; the shapes look so simple. *But* if it is not analysed and considered carefully, the result can look clumsy and crude. This is where the sometimes difficult job of simplification comes in: what is it about what you have seen that you want to capture? Perhaps fields could be simplified to bands of colour and texture, using short rows to make the stitches slant away from straight horizontals. Or, from a floral design, one flower could be extracted and repeated, or linked with some linear pattern that fits the knitting.

In theory, any design can be knitted: any shape, with curves, twists or angles, can be worked so as to fit the knitted fabric. But if the technique is considered and allowed to have a say in what suits it best, the result will be more satisfactory, easier to knit, and in the end will probably look more professional.

PLANNING

The best way to plan any sort of pattern before knitting it is to use squared paper, with one square per stitch, and chart it out, either in colours or symbols. It does not have to be to scale as long as you know what the tension will be when it is knitted, so that you know what size it will knit to.

If you are working out a single colour plain/purl textured pattern, or areas of colour as in intarsia, it is better to use knitting graph paper (see List of Suppliers) – the knitted stitch is wider than it is tall, so if ordinary squared paper is used, the design will appear taller on the paper, and come out disappointingly compressed when knitted. However, a jacquard pattern inevitably pulls in the widthways tension a little, and you might find your stitches do knit almost square in jacquard knitting (ie the same number of stitches and rows to a given measurement). In this case squared paper might give an accurate picture of the design, but do check this first before embarking on a large project. As a rough guide, in plain stocking stitch, 4 rows and 3 stitches form a square; but this does vary individually, and with different stitches.

Again, remember the following points when designing an all-over pattern, whether in texture, intarsia, jacquard or in any combination: in order to get a professional finish, the weight of the yarns and the distribution of the pattern must be planned so that the work makes a good all-over fabric; otherwise you will risk a lumpy, uneven finish.

ABSTRACT/RANDOM

Is all this planning and technical detail really necessary? You can surely just knit, introduce new colours or stitches when you feel like it and see what develops? Certainly, this is a very organic, spontaneous and exciting way to work: perhaps just a vague idea will spark you off and will evolve as the knitting progresses. The main danger is an uneven, buckled fabric with some bits sagging and others pulling in. The only way to avoid this is to learn how different yarns or stitches will behave, and/or do a certain amount of planning.

Some people prefer not to plan, even to the extent of having to undo large amounts of unsuccessful work rather than trying a sample first. You have to find a way of working that suits you; and it might be worth considering that, for the amount of time it takes to knit something, it must be worth doing enough planning to get the best possible result.

Abstract designs might appear to be spontaneous and random, but in order not to look clumsy or amateur they have to be carefully planned first.

PLACING THE PATTERN
ON THE GARMENT

Many traditional knitted garments would incorporate pattern partly as reinforcement, as a way of producing a thicker, stronger fabric on the parts of the garment that received most wear, such as edges, borders and cuffs. As these are also the parts that need to lie flat, this is another reason for using a decorative or different stitch at the edge if the main body of the garment is in stocking stitch.

As discussed earlier (see chapter 2), the extra thickness bestowed by patterned knitting very often also had a functional use: to make extra warm those areas such as the chest, back, shoulders and upper arms. This can be seen on guernseys and fishermen's sweaters, which were often in no more than plain and purl stitches; however, this still gives a slightly more textured, therefore warmer fabric, particularly if cables and cross-over stitches are used as well. The Scandinavians were more exuberant in their use of pattern for warmth and decoration, using colour more freely, often all over, with a change of pattern at the edge for borders.

So, the next decision we have to make is how or where to apply pattern to our design: whether to use it all over, or to draw attention to certain features, or where to place a large motif or shape. One attitude to decoration was summed up by the Victorian architect and designer, Pugin, when writing about design and ornament. Although he was referring to architecture, his observation makes an interesting starting point for designing in any field: 'all ornament should consist of enrichment of the essential construction'. This can be readily applied to handknitting, a structural technique where a whole garment shape can be 'built up', and where the maker is all too aware of the stress points and edges that can be strengthened by use of stitch decoration.

As handknitted garments can be created as a whole complete shape, and the fabric does not have to be cut as in dressmaking, the pattern does not need to be repeated continuously, regardless of the shape being knitted, but can be built into the design to fit the garment as required. There are various ways this can be done.

THE GARMENT STRUCTURE

It can be a daunting prospect, deciding where to begin, so why not start in the simplest way by looking at the structure of the garment, and using the seams, joins, fastenings or edges as the points to be emphasised by decoration? This can be extremely effective, and will give an expert finish to a garment. Even if the jumper or jacket is knitted

■ Placing the pattern on the garment:
a) emphasising edges, seams and borders
b) emphasising particular areas

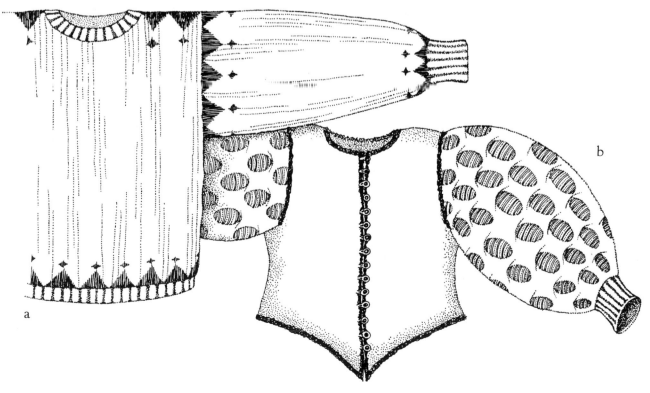

A jacket by Carol Wainwright, using jacquard and intarsia combined with textured stitches to form a repeating but varying pattern

in one piece, it gives a strong focus to make a point of joins such as armholes, shoulders, hems and cuffs. This can be done in the simplest way, by using a ridge of reverse stocking stitch, or a band of a textured stitch. The plainest guernsey has very simple, strong decoration, using only garter stitch, and 2 + 2 ribbing as decoration on a stocking stitch ground, with the added detail of a knotted-edge cast-on, which is both strong and decorative.

The idea can be developed with colour, still keeping it restrained: try using a different colour for all cast-on and cast-off edges, including shoulder seams, against a plain or textured background fabric. This has a similar effect to contrast piping on furnishings, and can look very smart.

Progressing from here, a small geometric pattern could be introduced, running along all these edges. This sort of decoration is very satisfying visually, perhaps because strong edges are important to the professional appearance of a garment; bringing attention to the edges makes them look bolder and stronger.

It is tempting to use an all-over pattern without considering positioning, and it is sometimes difficult to keep the design simple, especially if you are easily bored by plain knitting; but the result of a restrained design can be just as effective and sometimes more distinctive than an all-over pattern.

EMPHASISING THE MAIN FEATURE

Another approach to positioning a design is to bring attention to one main feature of the garment by means of pattern. For instance, very full, exaggerated sleeves could be decorated to make them the main feature, in contrast to a plainer body. Or a waist could be pulled in and emphasised with a patterned stitch; or frills, or a large collar could be made the main decorative emphasis, with coloured patterns or lace stitches on these parts. The same could apply to men's garments; looking again at traditional fishermen's designs, the main decoration could be on the shoulder panels, or across the chest and back of a sweater.

Try sketching a simple-shaped garment, and then patterning different areas to see how the emphasis shifts. Bolder, larger-scale patterns can be tackled in the same way: use a line drawing of a garment shape and divide it into different areas of colour; or place a large motif on the front or back and see how it relates to the shape, what shaped areas are left around it, and whether it enhances the shape of the garment or detracts from it. The scale of the pattern is very important in relation to the shape of the garment. Too small a pattern may be so dainty that it becomes hardly noticeable; too large and it can diminish the garment – or the wearer! Children's clothes are sometimes designed with adult-scaled patterns and they look clumsy on the smaller garments.

RANDOM DESIGN

The problem can be approached from another direction entirely: you can disregard the shape of the garment and let the pattern travel across it or settle at random, as if caught in transit. This makes a startling impact; it is less restful and satisfying visually than following and emphasising the shape of the garment, but it is far more unexpected and eye-catching.

This different approach in some way reflects the pace of life: a random design which is 'dropped' onto a garment has an immediacy and sense of haste about it – the fleeting, rushing, exciting feel of fashion, city life and crowds – whereas a pattern that follows the garment shape in a more traditional way has a timeless, studied mood, as though thought and consideration have been given as to how best to treat this particular shape. Of course this is all an illusion: just as much thought and planning have to be given to something that looks spontaneous and unexpected; and the more traditional approach can still be vigorous, lively, strong and full of movement, as is so well illustrated in William Morris's designs for fabrics, both printed and woven.

THE TEST OF CLOSE INSPECTION

Whichever way you approach designing, or whatever kind of effect you are aiming at, try to make a design where the added interest is afforded *because* it is knitted by hand: one of its qualities being that it is striking from a distance, but also grows in interest on closer inspection.

We see people both at a distance, as moving shapes, and in close-up. Clothes are to be seen from all angles and distances, as much from behind, in shops, streets and queues, as face-to-face in conversation. Furthermore, our eyes take in more at a glance than we realise, so a design can be immediately conspicuous from a distance even if it is not obviously dramatic or striking: it may be restrained and quiet, but it still catches the eye. However, the real test comes on closer inspection: does it then hold the interest and excite, or does the eye become bored and turn away? It should be possible in handknitting to give it enough detail, even if only in the beauty of the yarn or in the subtlety of shading or texture, to keep the interest when close up. Thus the design may be a simple arrangement of coloured stripes, but with textures only noticeable from close to; or it may be an all-over design, perhaps a small-scale pattern, which from a distance has the effect

A jacket by Yoshimi Kihara, with free-formed intarsia patterning incorporating mohair yarns

of a rich but plain orangey shade, while close up it is seen to be an exciting mix of bright reds and yellows.

ILLUSION AND FLATTERY

Another important use of pattern is to lead the eye in such a way that the design on a garment will flatter the figure. Obviously the garment's shape is important here, too, but the pattern can be used very successfully to create illusions. Shoulders can be made to look wider and stronger (conversely they can end up looking droopy); hips can look slimmer and waists longer, depending where the pattern is placed, and how it leads the eye.

The most obvious example of this is in striped patterns: there is no doubt that horizontal stripes make a figure look wider! If you want to use stripes in a pattern, and want to avoid this horizontal effect, the garment could be knitted across from side to side, so that the stripes hang vertically.

Bold patterns suit some people; others look better in softer, more detailed patterns. This is something else to consider and experiment with when designing. But it is the general direction of stripes that has the greatest effect. This can be used to advantage, not just by using the stripes vertically; a very flattering effect is to direct the pattern in diagonal stripes to a downward point at the centre back and front of a jumper. Try sketching this idea, then turn the 'chevron' the other way, sloping outwards from the centre, and see how it gives the illusion of the figure sagging and drooping from the shoulders.

EASE OF CONSTRUCTION

When you have decided the sort of pattern you want to knit, stop and consider which would be the *easiest* way to knit it. If it has vertical coloured stripes or bands using several colours, knit it across, sideways, with the bands falling down the garment. This means that you are knitting in more straightforward, horizontal banding, with fewer colours in a row.

If there is a diagonal direction to the pattern, then see if it would be simpler to knit a bias fabric by beginning at one corner, increasing at both ends of the row to begin with, to make the pattern slant, so that again it can be knitted in horizontal rows but will sit diagonally on the garment.

If the design changes from an area of horizontal patterning to a yoke with a vertical pattern, knit the yoke sideways as suggested before, perhaps joining it in one piece with the sleeves. Likewise, if any part of the garment has a pattern going in a different direction, see how you can divide up the construction into different areas. It need not mean extra seams if stitches are picked up from one edge and knitted on in another direction.

You may be working on a design which has large motifs, in which case decide whether jacquard or intarsia is suitable, so that you don't carry more yarns than you need across the fabric.

Work out the design on graph paper so that as few colours as possible are used in each row. This may mean continuing with a repeat a little longer before the next colour is introduced, but it will make the knitting much easier.

If you have decided on a design which does need several colours in each row, it is a good idea to avoid lots of balls of wool which are bound to get tangled. There are various ways of getting round this problem: either the yarn can be knitted in short lengths which are easier to untangle (use this for colours that only occur in small amounts, or there will be too many joins). Alternatively, small amounts of each colour can be wound on to bobbins, so that they hang at the back of the knitting and don't unravel until needed. Bobbins or yarn holders can be bought from suppliers, or can be made out of small pieces of card.

7

SHAPES AND DETAILS

Knitting clothes by hand gives enormous scope for experimenting with different shapes and styles, from simple to complex. Handknitted garments are 3-dimensional, where the shaping can be built into the construction, beginning from any given point and working in any direction; so it is possible to make clothes which fit closely and accurately, with curves and darts built into the fabric as it is knitted. If you want to make a garment fitting like a glove, or fitting closely in some places and full in others, the shaping can be worked into the knitting, and a whole garment created in one piece, without seams.

Mary Thomas wrote two invaluable knitting books published in the 1930s (see Bibliography) which are a great inspiration, and written with a deep understanding of knitting technique and its creative possibilities. In them she describes two separate methods of making knitted garments: one which she calls the 'peasant' method, where garments are built in one piece out of cylindrical tubes; and the second the tailored method, constructing each design from separate flat pieces carefully shaped to fit the body. Sixty years on, when fashion has broadened to encompass a wider range of shapes in everyday dress, it seems to me that these two methods need not be separated, but the shaping can be built into the three-dimensional structure, so using the technique of hand knitting to its maximum potential. There is no need to knit separate pieces which have to be joined later. The only reason I can think of for dividing a design into

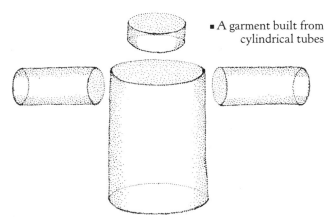

■ A garment built from cylindrical tubes

separate pieces (apart from reasons of technique such as intarsia patterns, mentioned in chapter 3 p47), even if the shape is extravagantly tailored, is that working on one section at a time (ie front, back, and separate sleeves) means that there is less shaping to think about in each piece: but then it has to be joined together afterwards, and there is not the enormous satisfaction of casting off the final stitches and having a whole garment completed by means of the knitting alone.

All the suggestions for designing in this chapter will look for the simplest way to construct each garment (which may not be the way that we have become accustomed to in most knitting patterns), and will presume that every item is knitted in one piece without seams, unless there is a reason given for doing otherwise.

BLOCK PATTERNS

One way to design the shape of a garment exactly to fit a particular figure is to make an accurate block pattern by taking certain measurements from the body it is to fit, as is usually done in pattern-cutting for dressmaking. Measurements are taken at given points of the body (chest/bust, waist, length of arm, etc) and drawn up on graph paper to scale, joining each point to make an outline of the body shape. Once the block has been drafted, tracings can be taken from it, and different designs drawn directly onto the tracings. Garments can then be designed and

made to fit very accurately. This would be particularly useful when designing closely-fitting, tailored garments for figures that are difficult to fit, for example with long waists, large busts, or narrow shoulders. It can be used for looser shapes as well, once you have decided how much to add to your measurements for a comfortable fit, which may vary according to the fashion of the moment. It is a foolproof method for getting the correct fit, but it does involve paper work and calculations before you can begin.

■ Shapes and details of garments

SIMPLER SHAPING

For a more spontaneous method of designing, there is a way of approaching the shaping and fitting problem from a different angle. If you are content to begin by designing garments that are simply constructed with minimum shaping, and not closely fitted, it is possible to use one very simple calculation to start with, on which a whole design can be based, and to progress to more complicated shaping and fitting later as your understanding develops.

After first calculating the number of stitches you will need, a great deal of the work can be done by eye and tape-measure. You could also experiment and try using the different stitches which shape the garment by pulling in certain areas (see chapter 4 p53), so that the number of stitches in use need not be altered – it is increasing and decreasing stitches that requires the most mathematics and preparatory paperwork.

CALCULATING FOR A SIMPLE JUMPER

(The instructions are for knitting in the round, with references to working in separate pieces as well).

Let us begin in the simplest way with a plain jumper: follow the directions below; shape variations are discussed later in this chapter.

1 **ESSENTIAL IN EVERY CASE,** even for the simplest shape, is to knit a tension sample in the pattern and yarn you have decided to use, at least 10cm (4in) square: the larger your sample is, the less room there is for error, as inaccuracies become magnified in the larger scale of the complete garment. The fabric can be as complicated as you like, it is the garment shape that needs to be simple to begin with.
Note: if you plan to use different stitches within the design, you will need a tension sample of each stitch.

2 Draw a sketch of the shape of your garment, laid out flat (see diagram).

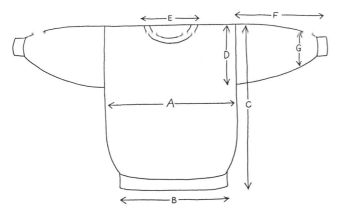

■ Simple-shaped jumper, showing the measurements needed for working out a written pattern

3 Measure a garment you have already that is a good fit, ie with the amount of tightness or looseness you want in your new design. Do not measure yourself at this point. Fill in the measurements on the diagram.

4 Measure your tension sample:
a) the no of sts to 10cm (or 20cm, or whatever size your sample is)=(X)
b) the no of rows to 10cm=(Y)
Measure 3 times in different places on the sample, and take the average if it varies: the smallest inaccuracy will be multiplied when transferred to the total stitches.

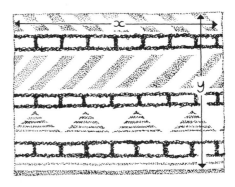

■ Measurements taken from a tension sample

5 To calculate the no of sts to cast on (this is simple with a calculator):
Divide the total measurement round the body (twice the flat width measurement) by the measurement of the sample, and multiply by the no of sts in the sample measurement (X) ie

$$\frac{\text{body measurement} \times (X)}{\text{sample measurement}} = \text{no of sts needed}$$

For example: if your model garment measures 66cm across the width (132cm round), and there are 18 sts to 10cm in your sample, your sum would be:
$$\frac{132 \times 18}{10} = 237.6$$

6 Look again at your tension sample. If it uses a pattern with a repeat, round the number of stitches up or down to make it fit the stitches round the body exactly. For example, your calculation tells you that you need

237.6 stitches; if your pattern has a repeat of 10, then round the number of stitches up to 240 stitches.

If the jumper is being knitted in separate pieces (ie back and front), it is less important that the pattern fits the stitches, as there could be a few spare stitches each side, next to the seam, to be knitted in an appropriate stitch that will blend, or contrast with the pattern.

If the pattern has a large repeat, it needs to be placed symmetrically.

7 The **body** is now knitted in the round, with your stitch-pattern adjusted as necessary for circular knitting, remembering that there are no 'wrong-side' or purl rows because knitting every round produces stocking stitch. So if your sample piece has been knitted back and forth, and you are following written instructions for the stitch pattern, the knits and purls need reversing in alternate rounds.
eg: a pattern that reads:
row 1) K3, P1, rep to end of row
row 2) K1, P3, rep to end of row
producing a 3 + 1 rib, would become 'K3, P1' in every round.

The length of the body can be judged by eye or measured, knitting it as long as you want, until the armholes are reached.

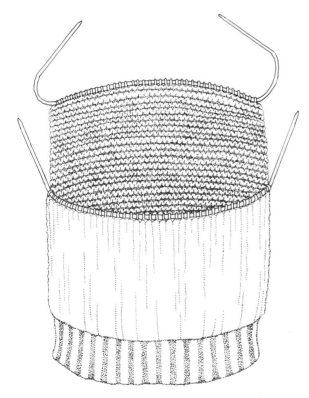

■ Knitting the simple jumper in the round to the armholes, then back and forth to the shoulder

8 Divide for the **armholes**, putting the stitches for the front on a spare circular needle or stitch holder. The simplest armhole is worked without shaping, making

a dropped shoulder line: carry on straight up the back, knitting back and forth. This can be continued on straight needles, or working back and forth on a circular needle. (Remember to adjust the knits and purls in your pattern on wrong side rows when working back and forth.) Work to the required length, completing the repeat in your pattern if necessary, then hold the stitches.

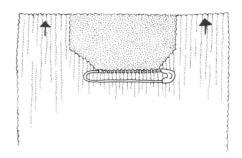

■ Simple round-neck shaping

9 **Front**: work straight until you reach the height for the front of the neck.

The simplest neck shaping is to work straight across as for the back, but that brings the neck very high at the front (as on the traditional guernsey). A more comfortable neck would be dropped to a curve at the front. To calculate: use the same formula described at the beginning to tell you how many stitches to leave on a holder for the base of the front of the neck:

$$\frac{\text{front neck measurement x (X)}}{\text{sample measurement}} = \text{no of sts for front of neck}$$

Now subtract neck stitches from total front stitches, and divide in two, to give the number of stitches for the front as it travels up each side of the neck.

Work out how wide the neck measurement needs to finish up, and do another calculation to tell you how many stitches you need to finish with on the front as it reaches the shoulder. Leave the remaining centre neck stitches on a holder, then work half the neck at a time, casting off one stitch at the neck edge every row until the right number of stitches is left. Work straight to match the length of the back.

10 Cast off **shoulders** together: place front and back stitches parallel, wrong sides together, and using a third needle, cast off through both, making a ridge on the outside. If you don't want the ridge to show, cast off right sides together, so it comes on the inside. The cast-off could be made a decorative feature by using a contrast colour.

The shoulder seam is always under strain as it carries the weight of the body and sleeves, and making a cast-off seam gives a strong join that will not stretch, and will hold the jumper in shape.

If you want an invisible join, graft the front and back together (see p97 'Joins').

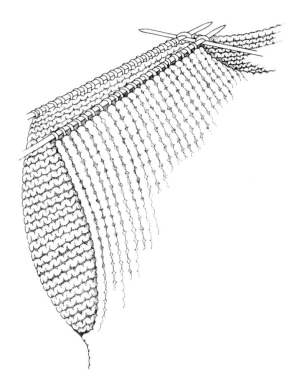

a) use the original calculation to work out the number of stitches for the top of the sleeve, which will be the same width as twice the armhole depth;

b) then work out the number of stitches for the bottom of the sleeve, above the cuff.

c) The top 10cm (4in) of the sleeve will be worked at full width without shaping to allow room for movement, so measure the length of the sleeve from 10cm below the armhole to above the cuff, as this is the length that will be decreased.

▪ Casting off shoulders together

11 Sleeves are knitted downwards, picking up the stitches round the armhole (which needs a circular needle, even if the sleeve is knitted back and forth). They can be knitted with no shaping, using the cuff to pull them in at the wrist. If the sleeve is very full, a shorter sleeve with a long cuff would keep the fullness out of the way.

However, a basic sleeve shape will probably narrow towards the cuff. For the simplest shaping:

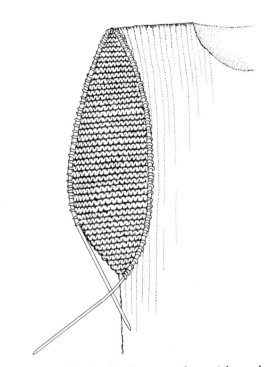

▪ Picking up stitches for the sleeve round a straight armhole

▪ Length to measure for decreasing the sleeve

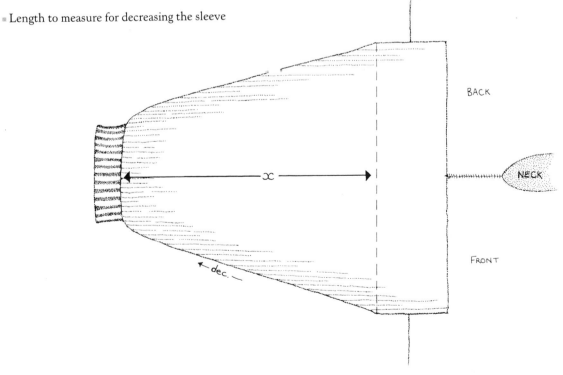

77

Calculate the number of rows in this length, by the same sum:

$$\frac{\text{sleeve measurement x (Y)}}{\text{sample measurement}} = \text{no of rows in sleeve}$$

d) subtract b from a = no of sts to decrease.

e) divide d in half = no of decreases. One stitch will be decreased each side of the sleeve seam (or imaginary seam if knitting in the round), so 2 sts are decreased each time.

f) divide c (no of rows) by e (no of decreases): this gives how often to decrease.

If it is not an exact number, round it up, as it is preferable to have the sleeve a little too wide at the cuff, rather than decreasing too fast and finding it too narrow.

Don't panic: You will probably find that you need to shape the sleeve about every four rows, and if the calculations are too daunting, try decreasing at this rate, bringing the sleeve in at the cuff to give a firm finish. The sleeve can either be made in the round, going onto four needles as it decreases and becomes too small for a circular needle, or knitted back and forth on a circular needle, leaving an underarm seam. (The circular needle is essential to get round the curve at the top of the armhole.)

g) *Cuff:* calculate the cuff measurement as before, but using a sample of the cuff stitch on the appropriate needles, which are usually a size or two smaller to give a firm edge.

Decrease evenly along the row to the required number of stitches, and knit the cuff.

12 Neck: Calculate the stitches needed round the neck by measuring the neck of your model jumper, and using a short circular needle in the appropriate size (see g), first thread on the stitches that are being held at front and back of the neck, then using the same circular needle, pick up and knit stitches along the slope of the front of the neck, up the side, and knit round the held stitches (see chapter 3 p40 for picking up stitches). Knit the neck in the round for as long as you want, remembering to keep the cast-off edge flexible enough for your head to go through.

Now you have a very simply-shaped jumper, with no seams to sew except possibly the sleeve seam. Following this method it is very easy to vary the shape, either by using different stitches, or by working out the number of stitches for increasing and decreasing for the shaping by the same formula as above, finding the position for the shaping by calculating the number of rows in the length.

Picking up stitches round the neck on a short circular needle

BODY SHAPES

Because of the stretch of knitted fabric, shapes can often be kept simple and still fit the body. However, even simple garments may need shaping in some cases to fit different people.

NARROW HIPS, BROAD SHOULDERS (or full bust)

a) calculate stitches for hip measurement
b) calculate stitches for top width.
To work out how often to increase, measure the length over which you will increase: probably up to the armholes will be adequate. Calculate the number of rows over this length. Subtract bottom stitches from top stitches, and divide by 4, because you will increase 4 sts each time (2 either side of each imaginary side seam). This gives the number of increases.

Divide the number of rows by the number of increases, to find out how often to increase.

When you begin knitting, mark with a tag of wool at each side point (imaginary side seam), and increase either side of the marker, which can be moved up as the knitting progresses, row by row.

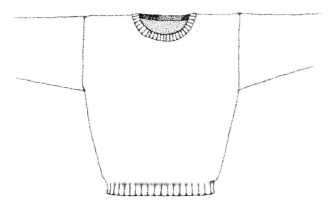

▪ Shaping for narrow hips and broad shoulders

You can make the increase decorative by using a contrast stitch at this point which also helps to mark the position, and increase either side of it: eg a purl stitch on a stocking stitch ground. If you are working in a pattern with a repeat, it might be difficult to incorporate the new (increased) stitches, in which case they could be knitted in a different stitch, emphasising the widening shape of the jumper. Alternatively, if this does not suit the design, work the pattern into the new stitches as invisibly as possible.

WIDE HIPS, NARROW SHOULDERS

Calculate as above in reverse, decreasing 2 stitches each side at intervals throughout the body.

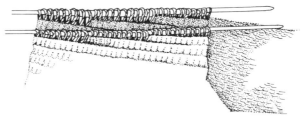

▪ Sloped shoulders can still be cast off together

SLOPING SHOULDERS

The shoulders can still be shaped and cast off together within this format of making a whole garment with no seams, by working 'short rows': when the height of the shoulder is reached, count the shoulder stitches and divide them into 3 or 4 groups. Work in the pattern to the shoulder edge, turn, and work back to the neck edge.

Turn, and work until you have one group of stitches left at the shoulder edge; leave them on the left hand needle without knitting them.

Turn and work back. Continue in this way, leaving another group of stitches unworked at the shoulder edge on alternate rows, but keeping the stitches on the needle.

When the last group of stitches has been worked, the back and front can be cast off together as before, making a sloped shoulder join.
Note: to avoid a 'step' in the shoulder shaping, slip the first stitch each time you turn, rather than working it.

SHOULDER VARIATIONS

Shoulder joins can be made more decorative by using a different pattern, such as ridge and furrow, or a contrasting coloured pattern (see Stitch Library) for the last part of the shoulders, either on the back, or front, or both. The join could be made in a contrasting colour, and for a more decorative effect, a fancy cast-off could be used, such as picot cast-off (see chapter 3 p38).

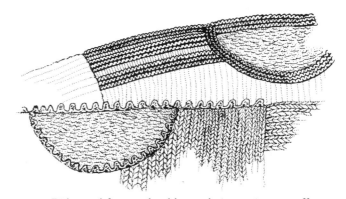

▪ Ridge-and-furrow shoulder, and picot-point cast off

LARGE BUSTS

In a simply-shaped design a large bust can be accommodated by enlarging the armhole, making it deeper, although this will also cause the sleeve to be wider. If it makes the sleeve too full, a gusset can be made under the armhole instead, to give more fullness – but the shape will still taper in so that the width of the sleeve is not affected. To make a gusset, begin a few centimetres below the armhole, and increase on alternate rows either side of the 'side seam' stitch until the armhole is reached. The stitches for the sleeve are then picked up round the armhole, with the gusset stitches included, and the sleeve knitted in the round, decreasing one stitch on either side of the gusset on alternate rounds until all the gusset stitches have been used up.

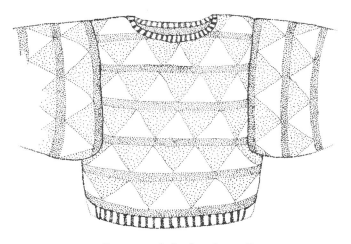

■ Deeper armholes for a looser fit

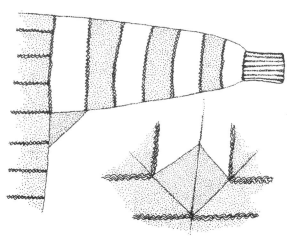

■ Underarm gusset

SHAPE VARIATIONS

CHEVRON

The whole jumper can be made an interesting shape while still keeping the number of stitches the same throughout and building the jumper on the same format; increase four stitches at each side, and decrease two stitches at the centre front and back at regular intervals, to make the shape dip down at the front and back in a chevron shape (see chapter 2 bias fabrics p27).

The tension is slightly different here, as the fabric produced is slanting to the diagonal, and the edge dips up and down. It will come out narrower than the same number of stitches worked straight, so you will need to allow more stitches to achieve the same measurement.

With this shaping, the centre front and back and side points need to be marked by dividing the total number of stitches into four, and using tags of wool or safety pins as markers. A double decrease is worked front and back, and a double increase at the sides, at regular intervals. For example, beginning at a side point:
Make one, pattern to 2 sts before front marker, S1, K1, psso; (front marker); K2 tog, pattern to 1 st before side marker, K into front and back of next st (side marker), M1; pattern to 2 sts before back marker, dec twice as for front, pattern to last st, K into front and back.

Shaping on alternate rounds gives a pronounced slope to the stitches, so a more gradual angle would be produced by shaping every 4 or 6 rounds. A small sample will show quite clearly how it can be varied.

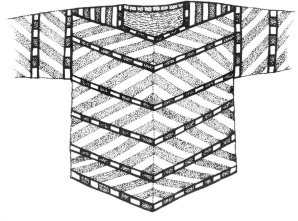

■ 'Chevron' shape made by increasing at the centre front and back, and decreasing at the sides, every few rows

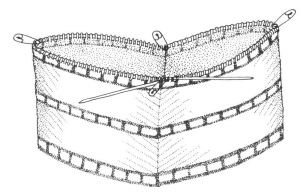

■ Mark the increasing and decreasing points with pins or tags of yarn

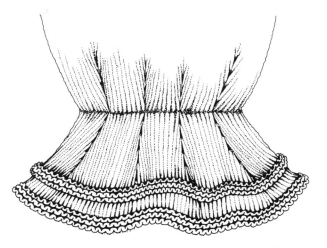

■ Decreases regularly placed round the jumper to shape into the waist

WAISTED SHAPES
■

To make a fitted waist to a jumper or jacket, stitches can be decreased and increased, using the original formula for calculating the number of stitches and frequency of the shaping. The decreases could be placed at intervals round the garment, perhaps using as few as four points, such as front, back and sides, and decreasing frequently in the rows. This would cause the bottom edge of the jumper to dip down in definite points where the stitches decrease, which could make an interesting feature of the design. Alternatively, if the decreases were placed at closer intervals regularly round the shape, they need not come so frequently in the rows, and could be staggered so that the effect would be of a smoother, more even decrease.

Another way of gathering in a waist would be to use a stitch that draws in, such as ribbing, cables, cross-over stitches, or 'woven' stitches (see Stitch Library). Samples would need to be tried with different stitches, to see whether they would gather in enough, or whether decreasing would be necessary as well.

A third way of drawing in a shape is to change the ten

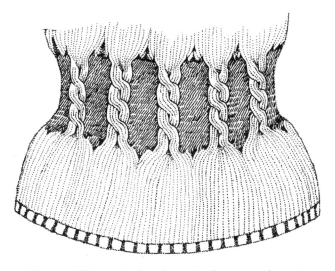

■ Using a different stitch to draw the shape in at the waist

sion, ie change to a smaller needle for the area that needs to be pulled in. This might not be suitable for every yarn, pattern or design, but is worth considering; and could be used in conjunction with either of the other two methods.

Sometimes it is difficult to decide what kind of edge or welt to use for a design. In this case you could cast on with a 'provisional cast-on' at the waist (see chapter 3 p39), above the planned welt, and pick up the cast-on stitches later to knit downwards. It is often easier to decide on the correct edge for the balance of the design when you have completed the rest of the garment and can see it in front of you.

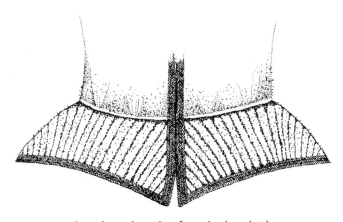

■ A peplum, shaped at front, back and sides

■ A frill (see Stitch Library no 40)

PEPLUMS
■

Peplums could be worked in this way, knitted down from the waist and casting off at the bottom edge, shaped either by increasing at spaced-out points, ie sides and middles of front and back; or by using a frill pattern which increases every few stitches, with the increases placed above each other either on alternate rows for a pronounced frill, or more gradually (ie every 6, 8, 10 or more rows) for a more gradual, gored effect (see Stitch Library no 41).

■ A frilled jacket designed by the author, knitted by Agnes Thompson

SKIRTS

This idea could be taken a stage further for knitting skirts or dresses, beginning from the waist and knitting downwards; in the case of dresses it is best to knit the top first, then pick up stitches round the waist and knit the skirt. It is easier to adjust the length in this way, as the skirt can be tried on with the waist fitting, and the stitches held on as many circular needles as necessary to spread out the fullness.

It is important to choose an appropriate good quality yarn that will not stretch, and a firm stitch that will hold the fabric in shape for a knitted skirt, or for any other large garment or fabric that is likely to carry a lot of weight. The danger for skirts in particular is for the shape to 'seat' with wear.

A good source of ideas for skirts is to look at knitting books from the 1930s–50s, when knitted skirts were popular. There are plenty of patterns using pleated ribbing (see Stitch Library) and the gored effect described above, together with other stitches which could be adapted for contemporary use.

Skirt and dress shapes that work successfully are either full, perhaps pleated or gathered, so that they hang well and the fabric can swing out; or an elongated sweater shape that is fairly full, and drawn in at the bottom edge. Anything closely fitted would be more likely to stretch and lose its shape.

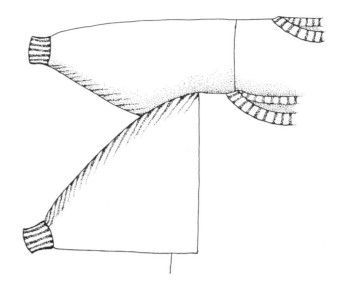

■ Decreasing sleeve under the arm and along the top of the sleeve

SLEEVES

We have already looked at the simplest sleeve which has no shaping at all, but is drawn in with a good firm cuff or suitable edging to give it a strong finish. The edge is important, or an unshaped sleeve can end up looking clumsy and unfinished.

Most sleeves are shaped gradually in towards the wrist, with the shaping along the length, under the arm. An alternative shaping which helps the sleeve to sit well on the arm is to decrease down the centre of the sleeve, along the top of the arm. This sets the sleeve at a sloping angle from the body rather than at right-angles as in the simple T-shape, but still uses a straightforward armhole shaping. It fits the body very well, with room for movement, but with no bulky fabric under the arm, as tends to happen on a full sleeve set in straight.

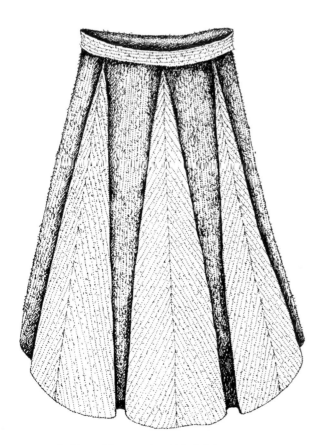

■ A skirt with gores (see Stitch Library no 41)

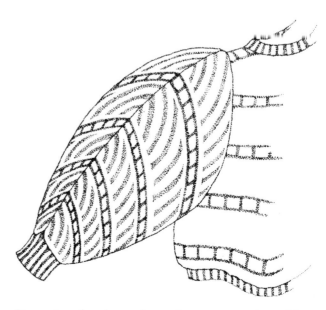

■ Decreasing the sleeve down the centre produces 'chevron' stripes in the pattern

The effect of this shaping on the knitted pattern is the same as on the 'chevron'-shaped body already described, as the knitted rows will fall at an angle at the point where the sleeve is decreased, which makes a decorative point of interest if the pattern has a stripe. The cuff will need to be shaped to fit this kind of sleeve, with a longer section in the middle, made by starting the cuff on a group of stitches in the centre, and working a few more stitches in at each side on every row until all the stitches are incorporated.

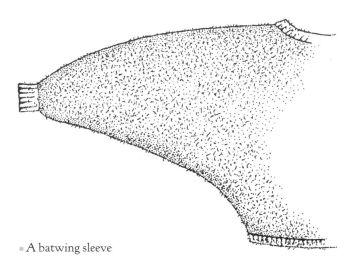

■ A batwing sleeve

A *batwing sleeve* which grows from a very wide beginning, even from shoulder to waist, may be shaped conventionally underneath, or again the shaping could be along the top, to make the sleeve slope downwards.

Still working in the format of picking up stitches round a straight armhole, the sleeve can be given more fullness by picking up extra stitches on top of the armhole. If it is difficult to pick up enough stitches for the fullness you want, make extra stitches in the following row by rapidly increasing, perhaps into every stitch to double the number of stitches at the top, or even increasing twice into some stitches, to give a gathered effect at the top of the sleeve.

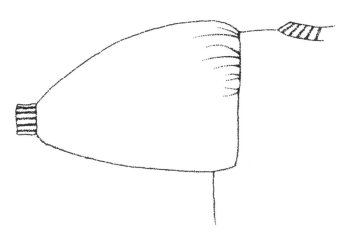

■ A fuller sleeve, with more stitches picked up at the top of the shoulder

Sleeves can be full, narrow, or shaped in or out down the length using the same way of calculating increases and decreases as the body; but much of the shaping can also be done by varying the length of the cuff.

CUFFS

If the cuff is to fit closely, it needs to be knitted in an elastic stitch, or else to have a button fastening, so the hand can go through. A wider cuff need not be stretchy as long as it uses a stitch that keeps its shape well. It could be finished with a hem, or a rolled stitch, or any other stitch that will retain its shape. Fancy edgings can also work well, such as a frill or a picot cast-off; or on a lighter-weight design, a lace stitch or moss stitch could be used.

1 Some **stretchy** stitches that make good cuffs are:
   a) ribbing: K1, P1; K2, P2; spiral ribs, or any rib-effect stitch
   b) welting, used sideways.
2 **Firm** stitches for non-stretchy, flat-lying cuffs:
   a) garter stitch
   b) jacquard, including 2-colour ribbing (this sometimes needs facing, see below and p24)
   c) slip-stitches
   d) bramble stitch (worked firmly on smaller needles) and similar stitches.
3 **Firm** stitches that **pull in:**
   a) woven stitches/alternate slip-stitches, such as slip-moss stitch
   b) cables, especially woven cable
   c) Tunisian knit or twice-knit stitches.
4 **Double** thickness:
   a) hemmed fabric, ie stocking stitch with facing folded in, or jacquard faced with stocking stitch
   b) tubular fabric (Stitch Library no 36 p119).
5 **Rolled edges:**
   Reverse stocking stitch allowed to roll back to form an edge.

ARMHOLES

Straight, set-in: A garment with no armhole shaping at all produces a dropped shoulder-line. The simplest way to lift the shoulder seam onto the shoulder is to cast off a few stitches at the beginning of the armhole, then work straight up to the shoulder. The number of stitches to cast off can be calculated by taking the measurement across the shoulders between the points where the seam is to be, and subtracting this number of stitches from the stitches for the back of the jumper. Divide these in half, to give the number to cast off at each armhole.

A simple shape like this will fit comfortably in most cases because of the stretchy nature of knitted fabric; a deeper armhole will give more room for movement if needed.

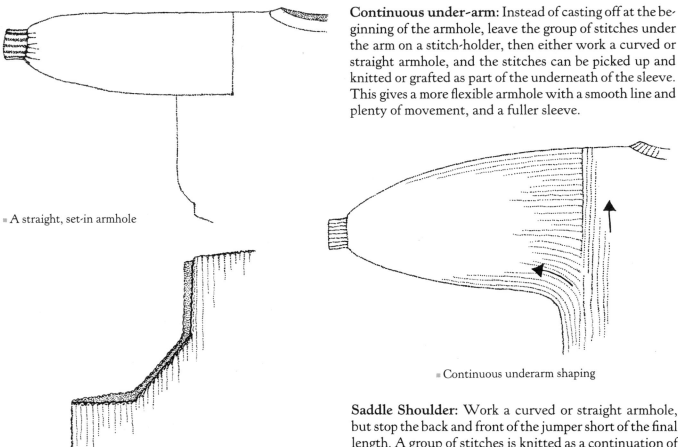

Continuous under-arm: Instead of casting off at the beginning of the armhole, leave the group of stitches under the arm on a stitch-holder, then either work a curved or straight armhole, and the stitches can be picked up and knitted or grafted as part of the underneath of the sleeve. This gives a more flexible armhole with a smooth line and plenty of movement, and a fuller sleeve.

■ A straight, set-in armhole

■ Continuous underarm shaping

■ Shaping for a round armhole

Round: For a closer-fitting, more tailored garment, a round armhole might be better, although it is more difficult to knit-in the sleeve; this will need a curved top to fit the armhole, and might be easier to knit separately and sew in afterwards.

Begin by casting off just a few stitches, in the same way as for the set-in armhole, but then decrease at the armhole edge every row until the required number is reached, making a curve instead of a corner.

Saddle Shoulder: Work a curved or straight armhole, but stop the back and front of the jumper short of the final length. A group of stitches is knitted as a continuation of the sleeve across the top of the shoulder:

a) If working the sleeve downwards, cast on a small group of stitches at the neck, work straight along the shoulder, then pick up round the armhole as before. The 'saddle' can either be sewn in afterwards, or knitted in to the back and front as it goes, at the end of each row.

b) Traditionally this shape has always been created by knitting the sleeve upwards: instead of casting all the stitches off at the top of the sleeve, a group in the centre is continued on to form the saddle shoulder.

■ A saddle shoulder

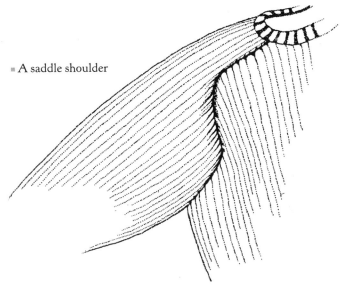

■ Cuff variations

Shapes and Details

Batwing: For a batwing shape, no armhole is formed at all – the sleeve is knitted as a continuation of the body, either upwards from the bottom of the body, increasing and casting on stitches for the sleeves; or knitted from cuff to cuff, again shaping gradually by increasing and decreasing, and some actual casting on and off when the shape grows or diminishes rapidly.

It is still possible to avoid seams in a batwing design, even if knitting a flat shape, by knitting as great a width as possible on a circular needle, and grafting the seams that have to be joined at the end. The seam to avoid in this shape is the shoulder seam, which would run down the top of the sleeve and could spoil the look of the whole garment. If the design is being knitted upwards from the bottom edge, knit over the shoulders and down the other side. If it is being knitted across, knit all the way from front edge to back edge on a long circular needle.

NECKS

Straight: The simplest neck is not shaped; the top seam simply left open for as wide as is needed for the head.

Square: The simplest way to shape the neck so that it is lower at the front is to calculate how wide it needs to be, and simply cast off this number of stitches when you reach the placing for the front of the neck. The stitches can be held on a stitch-holder so they can be knitted straight on for the band or collar. The sides continue straight up without shaping.

Round: A square neck is easily converted to a round one by casting off (or holding) fewer stitches at the centre front, then decreasing one stitch every row at the neck edge until it reaches the desired width. As in the curved armhole, this curves the corners of the neck. The back can be curved or straight, and the curve calculated in the same way.

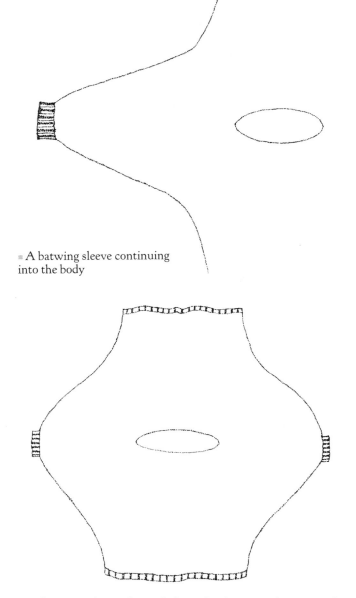

■ A batwing sleeve continuing into the body

■ A batwing design knitted from the bottom edge, over the shoulders and down the back, in one piece

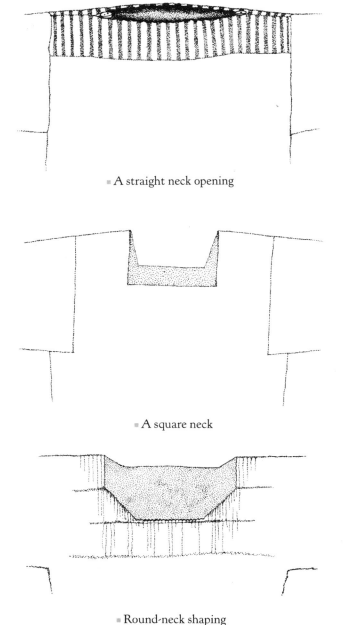

■ A straight neck opening

■ A square neck

■ Round-neck shaping

87

Scoop: Made in the same way as the round neck, only wider and more gradual.

V-Neck: This can begin at the same level as the armholes, or lower or higher according to the design. Leave one stitch at the centre on a safety pin for the base of the border, and work on one side at a time, decreasing at the neck edge every alternate or 4th row, depending on the depth of the V, and how wide it needs to be. It can be shaped part of the way up, then worked straight, calculating the number of stitches to decrease as usual.

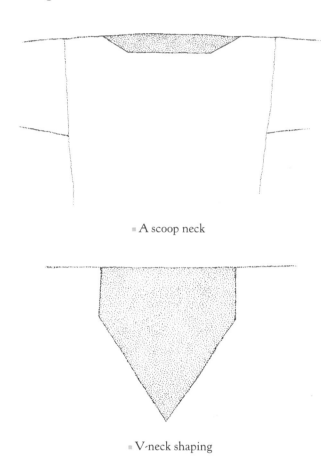

■ A scoop neck

■ V-neck shaping

Shawl collar: This can be fitted on a V-neck, or a V-neck with a flat base. For the second of these, cast off enough stitches in the centre to give the length of collar required, and decrease the sides as for the V-neck. If the collar is to be deep and wide, cast off a wider base and make an opening with straight sides.

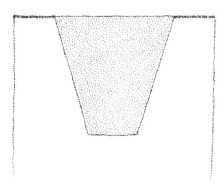

■ Neck opening for a shawl collar

COLLARS

Plain Bands and Polo Necks: Using a short-length circular needle, stitches can be picked up and knitted round any of the necks described above, using the stitches kept on holders at the front and back, and picking up from the sides as described in chapter 7 p78. A band can then be knitted in a suitable stitch for 2 to 3cm and cast off, or knitted for longer, and continued and turned back for a polo neck. Ribbing or other elastic stitches are ideal for neck bands, as they automatically draw in to make a neat edge. However, other stitches will work well giving different effects, including reverse stocking stitch which makes a rolled edge.

A band knitted onto a straight neck opening will make quite a high neck, which can be widened with the use of gussets at each side, like the guernsey.

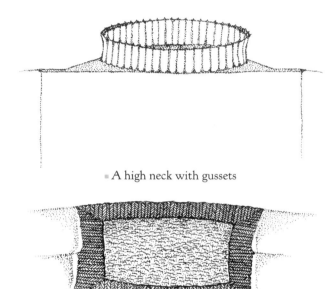

■ A high neck with gussets

■ A square neckband, decreasing at the corners

If the square neck is used, the neck band could be shaped by using a double decrease at each corner to make a definite angle and maintain the square shape, or the band could be knitted without shaping, in ribbing which will pull it in, to soften the corners.

A round neck makes a good basis for a plain neck band of any length, or for collars.

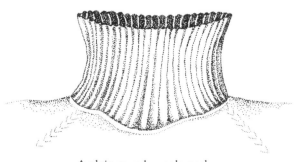

■ A plain round or polo neck

Shapes and Details

For the V-neck, the stitches are picked up round the neck as before, picking up the stitch left at the centre for the base of the V. Then two decreases are worked on every round, one each side of this centre stitch, thus:

S1, K1, psso K centre st, K2 tog, and cont round.

This rapid decrease makes a good sharp point to the V.

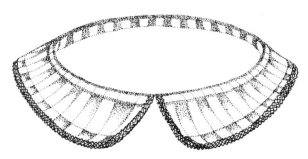

■ A rounded collar

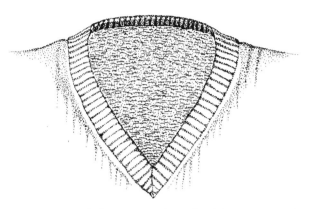

■ A V-neckband, decreasing either side of the centre stitch

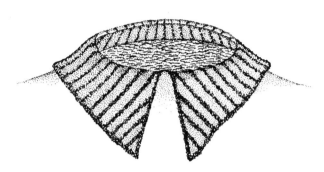

■ A pointed collar

Shawl Collar: Here the stitches are picked up along the sides and back of the neck, but not from the flat base of the front shaping. The collar is worked (usually in ribbing) until it is long enough to reach across the front flat base; then it is cast off and sewn down with the front edges overlapping.

For a more exaggerated shape, the increases can be more frequent, ie every row, making longer points at the front.

A collar knitted in a fairly stiff fabric (with a close tension) can be made to stand up, with increases at the centre back to match those at the fronts, shaping the collar away from the back of the head. It can be faced, to make a double thickness to help it stand up, decreasing the facing to match the increases of the collar.

The set of the collar can be changed by basing it on a V-neck rather than a round one, bringing it further down at the front.

■ A shawl collar in ribbed stitch

Divided Collars: A collar is begun in the same way as the round neck, picking up the stitches all the way round, but dividing it at the front (or back), and knitting back and forth (or work in two separate pieces with a division front and back).

Round collar: knit straight for a few rows, then decrease at the front corners to round them off, perhaps finishing with a knitted or crochet border all the way round the edge.

Pointed collar: In order to lengthen the front edges and to bring them further forward, stitches are increased on alternate rows at each front edge: either at the edge, or two stitches in, which makes a neat shaping.

■ A shaped collar, increasing at the centre back as well as front edges

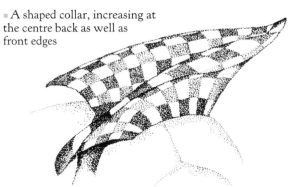

■ A shaped collar, as illustrated on p89 (bottom right), and turned back collar (by Carol Wainwright) showing reverse fabric

Fancy Collars: The bell frill makes an effective collar or decorative neck, knitted by increasing out to form a frill or ruff that will either stand up round the neck, or fall over, according to the length of the frill and the stiffness of the yarn and tension. Alternatively, it can be knitted the other way round, picking stitches up round the neck as before, and casting on extra stitches for the base of the frill as you go, then decreasing inwards to a round neck finish. This is more suitable for jackets than jumpers, as the cast-off edge will not readily stretch over the head (see Stitch Library).

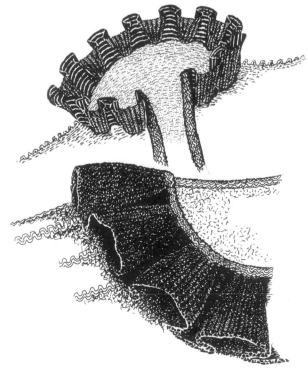

■ A frilled collar, worked two ways

Necks and Bands on Jackets: The neck and front bands can be picked up all in one, all the way round the edge, on one or two long circular needles, working from the bottom edge of one side, up the front, round the neck, and back down the other side. If the neck needs to be deeper than the front bands, short rows can be worked on the neck area only, building it up to the required height.

If there is an angle at the corner of the neck, the band can be increased at the corner to shape it round, or the front bands and neck band can be worked individually (see p40 and 93 for front bands.)

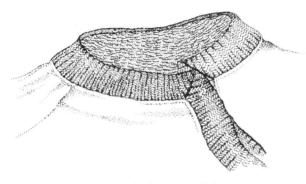

■ Neck and front band picked up round the edge, increasing to shape the corners

OPENINGS
■

This section will look at some of the simplest ways to build openings into designs which are knitted in one piece.

The most straightforward and accessible opening for a jacket or jumper is at the front, but this is also the most noticeable place to have an interruption to the design, as it cuts through the front of the garment. A more discreet opening could be made at the side seam, so that the front is not disturbed, but this is less convenient to fasten. Children's garments often need extra space for the head to go through, as children's heads are so much bigger than adults' in relation to their body size. For a jumper, a short front opening could be used, or a shoulder opening which fastens along the seam, and so does not interfere with the design.

■

Necks and front bands.
Left: neck band knitted first in K2, P2 in two colours with a facing, then front bands picked up and knitted in the same way; *centre:* band picked up all round edge and folded over; *right:* small reverse stocking stitch band (purl side out), picked up all round edge

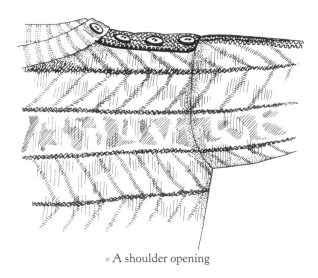

■ A shoulder opening

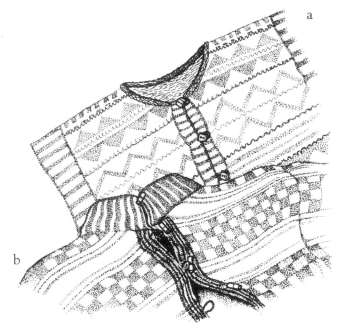

■ Edge-to-edge front openings, with a) bands picked up and knitted, and b) the band knitted vertically and sewn on, fastened with loops and buttons or toggles

Short front openings: If the design is a jumper with a close-fitting neck, it will be necessary to have a short front opening to let the head through, rather like an old-fashioned vest. There are examples existing in museums of beautifully fine 17th-century knitted vests using this form of opening.

A simple slit can be left in the knitting by dividing the front in two and knitting half at a time, with an edge-to-edge fastening of loops and buttons to finish off. The edge might need a narrow border to make it firmer and to give a better finish; or it could be faced with a strip that is picked up, knitted and sewn back inside the garment. The bands must be narrow, or the fabric will be distorted at the base of the opening.

ation of the front edge. In this case it would be important to match the two edges, as one front may be at the beginning of the work (ie cast on), and the other at the end (cast off). There would be two ways of dealing with this: firstly, you could make one band by casting off, and match the second front by casting on with a 'provisional' cast-on, then at the end pick up the stitches and knit the second band, with a cast-off edge to match the first band.

Or, the second front could be made by beginning with a 'cast-off' cast-on, to match the first, cast-off edge (see chapter 3, p39).

If the fronts have been knitted vertically, again, there would be two ways to proceed: first, the band can be knitted separately, in the same direction, and sewn on

■ A short front opening, as in this silk vest worn by King Charles I

Edge-to-edge front opening: This is the simplest way to fasten a jacket, as buttonholes are not necessary. A front edge opening to a jacket that has been knitted vertically will need front bands, to firm up the tension and give a finished look to the garment. If the jacket has been knitted so that the fabric is used sideways, the band can easily be knitted as part of the main garment, as a continu-

■ A band knitted upwards with vertical buttonholes

later. This gives a good firm edge, especially if knitted on smaller needles than the body of the garment, and the length can be measured as it is made, or it can be sewn on as it is knitted, to ensure a good fit.

Alternatively, stitches can be picked up along the edge and the band knitted sideways. This requires a little more care as the tension must be right, but it is satisfying to build the band on by knitting rather than sewing.

If ribbing is used, the elasticity of the stitch will help it to adjust to fit the front edge; but if the band is to be made in a flat stitch, then ideally a tension sample should be made using the appropriate needles and stitch, so that the correct number of stitches to be picked up can be calculated. The length of the front edge must be measured: the most accurate place to measure is a little way in from the edge, as the edge is often looser than the main fabric, and will need to be pulled into shape.

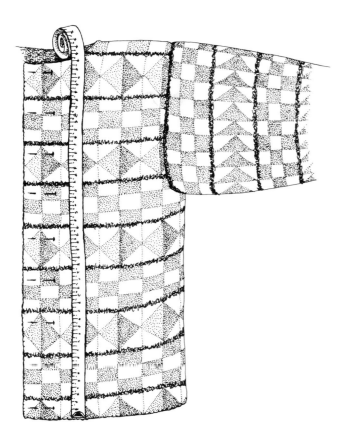

■ How to measure for picking up a front band, marking equal distances to help pick up stitches evenly

Calculate the number of stitches to pick up in the usual way (see beginning of this chapter), and mark with pins along the front edge, at the halfway and quarter points, so that stitches are picked up evenly. If the fabric is patterned, work out how many stitches to pick up to each repeat. See chapter 3 for picking up stitches, and then knit your band, making a facing if necessary for extra strength, and to prevent curling. Front bands must not pull in too much, or push out either, as this will spoil the front of the jacket.

Beware of picking up stitches unevenly (ie more at one end than the other), as this will distort the pattern on the front of the jacket so that it does not match up.

If the bands need fastening, buttons or toggles with crochet loops can be used to bring the edges together. If a closer, firmer fastening is required, a zip could be used, if the weight of the knitted fabric is suitable. Zips are by nature rather rigid and stiff, and not sympathetic to the character of knitted fabric, so would only be appropriate on a garment in a fairly firm stitch; they would need to be sewn on with care, without stretching or buckling the knitting.

Overlaps: A small overlap can be made with bands knitted as for edge-to-edge openings, and buttonholes made in one band (see p94). In this case, the jacket fronts can be the same width as half the back, so they overlap only by the width of the bands.

For a bigger overlap, the fronts will need to be made wider, calculating the width of each front in the original plan for the design. Buttonholes might need to be made in the main front piece of the jacket rather than just in the band, particularly for double breasted designs.

DIAGONAL: The fronts could be shaped in a more elaborate way, with the top wider to make a diagonal cross-over fastening; or the bottom wider so that the fronts cross each other in a complete wrapover shape. The shaping of the fronts would need to be planned and calculated as before, and incorporated into the overall shape of the whole garment. If a wrapover fastening is to be used, slits could be made in the knitting at the side seam point, so that ties could be threaded through for fastening.

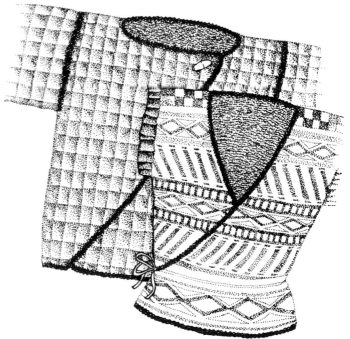

■ Diagonal and cross-over front openings (see photograph on p70 for an example of tie-fastening)

Side-Fastenings: A side opening could be made in the same way as the front openings, and edged according to whether or not it is to be a noticeable part of the design. If both sides open, this could become a decorative feature with fastenings playing an important role, for example tie-fastenings, or loops and decorative buttons. A side-fastening will alter the overall structure of the garment, and the order in which it is knitted, but it will still be possible to plan so that it is made all in one piece, either by knitting up and over the shoulders, and down the back; or sideways from cuff to cuff across the garment.

Shoulder Openings: A shoulder fastening is going to be visible, so needs to be made neatly, and faced or bordered so that it has a firm finish without being lumpy. It could be incorporated as a decorative feature of the design, either on one shoulder, or more symmetrically with a fastening on both shoulders.

BUTTONHOLES AND LOOPS

When deciding on the right fastening for your design, you have to consider the weight of the fabric, particularly the front band, as well as the look of the design. If you are using buttons, they need to be the right size and weight for the weight and thickness of the fabric; and the buttonholes must be as neat and strong as possible.

LIGHTWEIGHT FASTENINGS: For a fine, lightweight fabric, either loops or buttonholes could be used, and the button-band must be strong enough to hold the weight of the buttons. If the fabric is very fine, a very small circle of thin cloth could be sewn on the back of the band to strengthen the point where the button is to be attached.

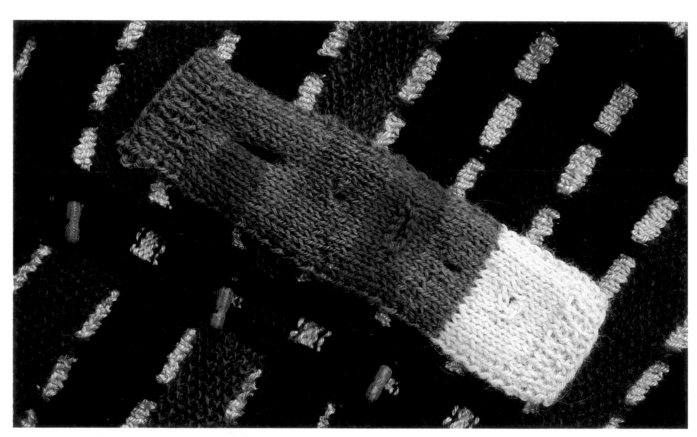

Inset: **Buttonhole samples** (from white end):
1 **Cast off 2 sts, and cast on 2 in following row** (thumb-twist method)
2 **Yarn over, K2 tog**
3 **1-row buttonhole:**
   Work correct no of sts to buttonhole position
   Bring yarn to front of work, slip 1 from LH needle to RH needle, pass yarn to back of work, and drop it
   * slip another st from LH needle to RH needle, pass 1st sl st over 2nd to cast off 1st st. Rep from * until required no of sts are cast off
   Slip last cast off st back onto LH needle. Turn work
   Pick up the hanging yarn and pass it between needles to the back. Using cable cast on, cast on 1 more st than you cast off, but do not place last st on LH needle yet. Bring yarn back

through to the front between last 2 sts, put last st on needle. Turn work.
   Slip end st from LH needle to RH needle, then cast off extra cast on st over it. Work to end of row.
4 **Reinforced eyelet:**
   Work to position of buttonhole
   Yo, front to back, cont row
   Next row, sl the yo, make another yo
   Next row, sl st before yos, K yos tog keeping on LH needle
   Cast sl st off over st just made
   K3 tog: yos and next st
5 **Vertical buttonhole:**
   Split work and knit one side at a time, for length required.
   Break off one end, and work across slit, weaving in the finished end as you go.

■ Front fastenings, showing loops and toggles, and buttonholes.

a) The smallest buttonhole is made by the 'hole' commonly used in lace patterns: K2 tog, yarn over; or Y O, K2 tog; with the Y O making the hole.

b) Another, slightly larger hole is made by casting off 2 sts in one row, and casting on 2 in the following row to replace them. The best type of cast-on for this method is to make loops over the left thumb and place them on the right-hand needle, as this continues the direction of the stitches being knitted, with no need to turn the needles (see chapter 3 p39).

Vertical Buttonholes can be made by making a split in the knitting for the length of the hole required. A separate yarn will be needed for each side, and when it is joined at the top, the second yarn can be woven across to strengthen the top of the hole, and the bottom end sewn in to do the same.

FASTENINGS IN HEAVY, THICK FABRICS: If the front band has a facing, it will be necessary to make a buttonhole in the band, matching it with another in the facing then sewing them together, perhaps strengthening the edges of the hole in the process with a sewn buttonhole stitch. This could end up rather thick and bulky, and it may be better to use crochet loops on the edge of the band rather than making a hole.

Crochet loops: First sew the buttons in place, then using a crochet hook slightly smaller than the size of the knitting needles used, make single chain on the edge of the opposite band to form a loop to correspond with each button, first making sure that any pattern on the fronts matches up. It strengthens the loop if the loose end of the yarn is used as a core to the chain, weaving it in and out as you make the chain, then sewing both ends in securely.

POCKETS

A pocket can be thought of as another three-dimensional shape to be built into a garment as it is knitted. There are several different ways of making pockets, but the basic components are an opening which can be either horizontal, vertical or diagonal, leading into either a patch or a loose pocket; and edged with a border or flap.

As we have seen, stitches can be picked up and knitted in any direction, either from the surface of the fabric, or from a selvedge or opening, so there is a wide choice of methods for constructing the pocket.

Once again it is important to look at the weight of the fabric you are using, to consider whether it is strong enough to support a pocket, and to decide which type of pocket would be most suitable for the kind of use it will have, as well as how it will look as part of the design. A lightweight garment might only need one small pocket, and a single patch pocket would be the least bulky on a fine fabric; whereas a heavy jacket could carry two good-sized pockets strong enough to accommodate having hands buried in them.

The main dangers are making a pocket that is too heavy so that the fabric becomes pulled and distorted at the opening; or making a patch pocket on the inside where the sewn edges show too obviously on the right side, and where if it were overfilled, again the garment would be pulled out of shape.

There are several ways of constructing pockets, and the following are a few suggestions:

■ A horizontal pocket opening with patch pocket, and inside showing free-hanging pocket

Horizontal Opening: Work to the place where the pocket opening is to be, and leave the required number of stitches for the pocket on a holder, to be used later for the border. For both a patch or a separate pocket, either:

1 knit the lining first, a single length for a patch pocket, or a double length to be folded back for a separate pocket; insert the top of this piece in the following row to fill the gap where the front stitches are being held, knitting them into the row and continuing the pattern. Or:

2 when you reach the pocket stitches in the next row cast on stitches (provisional cast-on would be ideal – see chapter 3 p39) over the slit where the front stitches are held, and continue the pattern, picking up from the cast-on edge to knit the lining downwards, at the end.

In either 1 or 2 the front stitches on the holder can be picked up and knitted as a border afterwards, with the edges sewn down, and the pocket lining sewn either to the back of the fabric (patch), or the sides sewn together to form a pouch separate from the main body.

3 Another method which could be used, depending on the pattern of the fabric, is to begin at the bottom edge of the pocket by increasing in every stitch to be used for the pocket, doubling the number of stitches over the pocket area. These are then worked in tubular knitting (see Stitch Library no 36), making a double fabric (which would knit up at the width of half the stitches, as half form the back of the pocket), until the pocket is

the height required. The front stitches can be held to be used for a border, or cast off, and the back stitches incorporated into the main fabric, as before.

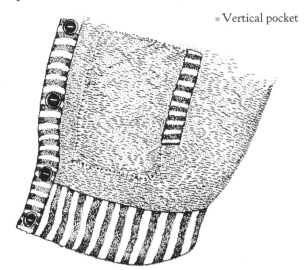

■ Vertical pocket

Vertical Pockets: Leave a slit for the opening by working each section separately. The edge nearest the side seam will have stitches picked up along the edge and a piece knitted sideways to form the patch on the inside. The edge nearest the centre front can be picked up to knit a border, with the corners sewn down.

If the pocket is placed in the side seam of a jacket or skirt, a separate (rather than a patch) pocket could be made, picking up the stitches as described above, and casting on extra stitches at the lower edge to make the pocket deeper. The lining piece is knitted and doubled back, as for horizontal pockets.

Diagonal Pockets: A diagonal opening is also made by dividing the knitting for the opening. Put all the stitches nearest the side seam on a holder (or leave them on a spare circular needle), and work on the stitches nearest the centre front, casting off one or more stitches on alternate rows at the pocket edge to make a slope. When the height of the pocket is reached, return to the stitches left

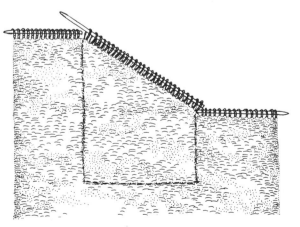

■ A diagonal pocket: hold sts at lower edge, work diagonal shaping, and pick up sts along edge to knit pocket band. The patch pocket is sewn on to the inside

at the lower edge, and the knitting is continued, either making the facing while knitting up by casting on extra stitches to go behind the opening, or knitting a separate facing first and joining it in at this point. In this case, the inside of the opening must be sloped to match the front edge, by increasing so that it is parallel with the first side.

When the top of the pocket is reached, the rows are worked all the way across again. A diagonal pocket can be edged with a border in the same way as a vertical pocket.

Flaps and Borders: A border is knitted on the front edge of the pocket, as described, in horizontal, diagonal or vertical openings. Several stitches would be suitable, including ribbing, garter stitch, reverse stocking stitch, or a small piece to match the welt of the garment.

A flap is only appropriate for horizontal pockets as it hangs over the front edge; it is made by picking up the stitches from the back (or top) of the opening, and working in a flat, non-curling stitch, or a double fabric.

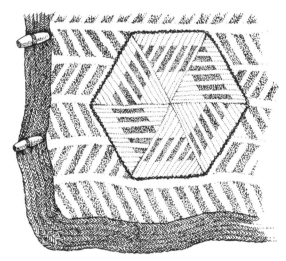

■ A decorative patch pocket on the outside

Patch Pockets attached to the Front: Patch pockets used on the outside can be any shape – circular, hexagonal, square, diamond, rectangular, triangular – and can be incorporated as a feature in the overall design; they can either be made separately and sewn on with the opening left unattached, or with stitches picked up and knitted from the main fabric. In this case, the sides can be knitted into the backing as you go, or sewn or crocheted on afterwards.

JOINS
■

Even if you aim to construct your design in one piece, there may well be seams that need joining, facings to be sewn back or pockets to finish off. A knitted garment can be ruined by the wrong kind of join, or one that is badly executed. Different stitches are appropriate for different joins, depending on the weight of knitted stitch and yarn, and whether the join is a seam or a hem.

When knitted fabric has the advantage of being made with finished selvedges at every edge, it seems a pity to turn these edges to the inside and make bulky seams: it is more logical to join them as smoothly as possible, edge to edge. However, this does depend on having very strong, neat selvedges; if there is any weakness, it may be necessary to make the join a stitch or two in from the edge.

If you want to avoid sewn seams altogether, there are two other ways of joining pieces: invisibly, by grafting the edges together; or by making a strong, visible, decorative join by crocheting together.

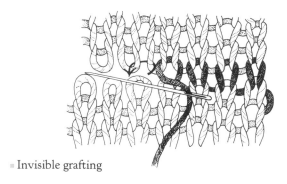

■ Invisible grafting

Grafting: This can be achieved either by using knitting needles, and breaking off the yarn so it can be pulled right through the stitches by the knitting needles; or it can be sewn with needle and yarn.

The knitting method is only appropriate if the pieces to be joined are knitted stitches, ie the top edge of a piece of knitting that has not been cast off. The row of grafting imitates a knitted row, working through both sets of needles, making a row in between indistinguishable from the rows of knitting, so that no join is visible. The stitches can be made knit-wise or purl-wise, according to the pattern of the knitting (see Bibliography).

This can also (perhaps more easily) be performed with a sewing needle and thread. The stitches can still be formed knit-wise or purl-wise, and can be used to join a side edge to a top or bottom edge as well, working into the side loops in the same way as the stitches.

Traditionally grafting has always been used for the toes of socks and stockings to make a smooth toe join with no ridged seam, but it has many contemporary uses too: for example an invisible shoulder join, or an invisible side seam in a jumper that has been knitted across sideways from cuff to cuff.

It can also be used in alterations or repairs, if a section of a garment has been removed and a new one inserted, and can be made over a larger area as invisible darning.

Crocheted Joins: These can be decorative if made in a contrast thread, but stands out anyway as strong ridges if the background colour is used, making the joins a prominent part of the whole garment.

If a contrast colour is used, it makes a neater join to work a line of single crochet along each of the edges to be joined first, working from the right side of the fabric.

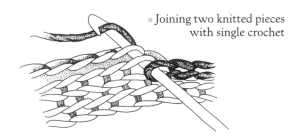

■ Joining two knitted pieces with single crochet

These edges can then be joined by single crochet, or double for a more pronounced effect; or any fancy stitch such as picot, to make a decorative seam. If the edges are crocheted together without the preliminary line of single crochet, one edge will have the stitches showing through from the back, giving a 'wrong side' effect.

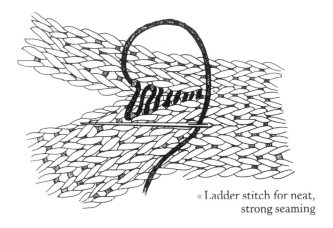

■ Ladder stitch for neat, strong seaming

Sewn Seams: The stitch that gives the strongest, neatest and least visible join, edge to edge, is ladder stitch, which can be made on the right or the wrong side of the knitted fabric. Ladder stitch is stronger than oversewing the edges, because it picks up from the top bar of the knitted loop rather than from the side edge, which can easily pull out and become loose. It draws the edges of the knitting firmly together, making an almost invisible seam; and has the added advantage of being slightly elastic, because of the zig-zag movement of the stitches, which closely follow the shape of grafting, and therefore of knitted stitches (see diagram).

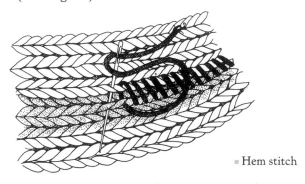

■ Hem stitch

Hem or Slip-Stitch: The other most useful sewn join is hemming or slip-stitch, used for joining an edge onto a surface, ie a hem, a pocket top, or perhaps catching down a rolled edge. It is not as strong as the other joins described, so is not suitable for seams or anywhere that will be under strain.

8

STITCH LIBRARY

This library is intended as a reference section, illustrating how knitted stitches can be used to make different kinds of fabric as well as visual patterns. It gives examples of a wide range of stitches, which could be copied exactly as they are shown, or modified to create different patterns, textures and colour effects. If you have an idea for a garment or other knitted fabric of a particular weight, this section can be used for reference to help you choose appropriate stitches.

Several well-known stitches are included here, but some of them have been used in colour combinations in such a way that the original character of the stitch is altered, creating something entirely new. For instance, when worked in a single colour, a certain stitch may have a pronounced textured pattern which will become lost if a combination of different colours is used, and new patterns and textures will emerge. Samples nos 32 and 34 will show how coloured stripes or jacquard effects, for example, can transform certain stitches. In the same way, a basic stitch such as ribbing, which is known for its stretchiness, will form a flat-surfaced pattern when worked in a jacquard technique with two colours to each row (see nos 22 and 23). Although photographs can give a clear idea of the look of each piece, and the text can tell you something about the feel and drape, the true character is only revealed in the handling of the fabric – and understanding why each stitch has its own particular characteristics comes through the constructing process: no amount of words can replace the experience of knitting it! If time is spent exploring the possibilities, new ideas for designs will begin to emerge. In this way, the illustrations can be used as starting points for the development of your own ideas.

A coding system has been introduced as a guide to the type of fabric which results from any particular stitch – whether it is thick or thin, firm or limp, whether it curls or lies flat – so that if a certain character of fabric is required for a design, reference to the symbols will indicate which stitches would be suitable. The physical characteristic of a stitch will also depend on the type of yarn and the size of the needle, so if your trial samples do not resemble the illustrations, try using larger or smaller needles, or different yarns.

My aim with this stitch library is to demonstrate how a combination of knit, purl, slip or cross-over stitches used sometimes in conjunction with colour-knitting techniques can produce fabrics of widely differing handling qualities. For this reason only a few stocking stitch jacquard patterns have been included, and no intarsia. Any design worked in stocking stitch using different colours to create the patterns, whether geometric, floral or abstract, can be worked out on graph paper. They may be copies or adaptations of designs seen in printed fabrics, embroidery, ceramics, graphics etc, as discussed in chapters 5 and 6, or they may be original designs; but it is easy to visualise the effect of a flat-colour pattern from a chart, and written instructions are not really necessary. Most of the samples in this library are derived from a combination of different stitches giving additional characteristics such as stretch, drape, and density; and can be used as a beginning to further exploration of how knitting techniques can be used in designing not just visual patterns, but whole fabrics.

All instructions are given for samples knitted back and forth, so if knitting in the round, exchange the knits and purls on even rows; ie garter stitch will become: knit 1 round, purl 1 round – instead of: row 1) knit, row 2) knit. Stocking st will become: knit every round.

ABBREVIATIONS		SYMBOLS USED IN THE CHARTS	
K	knit	⊡ knit on right side rows	
P	purl	⊡ purl on wrong side rows	
C	cable	⊟ purl on right side rows	
S	slip	⊟ knit on wrong side rows	
Slp	slip 1 purlwise		
st	stitch	⟋ K2 together	
st st	stocking stitch (knit 1 row, purl 1 row)	⟍ K1, S1, psso	
yf	yarn forward	⟱ S2, K1, p2sso	
yb	yarn back		
yaf	yarn at front	⟨S⟩ S1 with yarn at back (right side)	
yab	yarn at back		
O or YO	yarn over needle (makes an extra st when worked in following row, leaving a hole)	⟨s⟩ S1 with yarn at front (right side)	
tog	together	⟨ᴄꝛ⟩ Cross 2 left	
alt	alternate		
K1b	knit 1 into back of stitch	⟋⟋ K3 tog	
P1b	purl 1 into back of stitch		
psso	pass slipped stitch over	⟋⟋ K1, P1, K1 into 1st	
M1	make one by picking up bar from row below	⟨O⟩ Yarn over	
beg	beginning		
col	colour	⟨Ꙩ⟩ Knit thro back (purl thro back on wrong side rows)	
cont	continue		
inc	increase	⎿⎾ K st from row below, then next stitch	
dec	decrease		
		⟍ K st, then K st from row below	
FABRIC CODING			
⟩⟨	pull in	⟋⟋ Cable 4 (2 over 2)	
△	pull up		
⟨⟩	push out	∧ Cast on	
[ ]	thick		
O	open	⟩ Cast off	
/	bias		
~	stretchy	● Make bobble	
—	flat (non-curling)		
I	no stretch		

1 GARTER STITCH
△ [ ] —

Knit every row.

For clear-colour stripes, change colour on right side (odd) rows; for mixed-colour stripes, change colour on even rows. Changing colour every row makes a reversible pattern.

Sample a) shows a 3-colour pattern, with 1 row of each colour, worked on a circular or double-ended needle (to enable sts to be slid back and knitted in the same direction in following row):

G = grey, T = turquoise, B = blue

row 1: G, K, slide sts back
row 2: T, P, turn
row 3: G, P, slide
row 4: B, K, turn
row 5: G, K, turn
row 6: T, K, slide
row 7: G, P, turn
row 8: B, P, slide; repeat

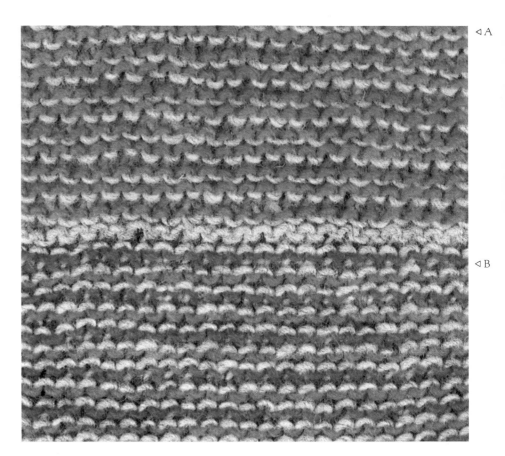

◁ A

◁ B

Sample b) shows 1-row stripes in 2 colours:

row 1: G, K, turn
row 2: T, K, slide
row 3: G, P, turn
row 4: T, P, slide; repeat

2 MOSS STITCH
<> △ —

Cast on an odd no of sts:
row 1: K1, P1, rep to end, K1
rep for every row

a) For a mixed colour effect, change col every row, using a circular or double-ended needle, sliding the sts back if the yarn is the wrong end.

b) For soft stripes, change colour on alt rows, making 2-row stripes.

c) **Alternate Colour Moss Stitch** >< △ [ ] —

Work as for moss st (see above), with 2 colours: one always used for knit, and one for purl.

The effect changes if the colours are swapped round.

◁ A

◁ B

◁ C

◁ D

d) **Slip-Moss Stitch** >< △ [ ] — I
Odd no of sts
row 1: K1 * S1p, K1, rep from * to end
row 2: K1, * yf, S1p, yb, K1, rep from * to end
row 3: K2, * S1p, K1; rep from * to last st, K1
row 4: K2, * yf, S1p, yb, K1 rep from * to last st, K1
rep these 4 rows
This st is very effective using different colours, changing either every row, or alternate rows, and makes a firm, thick fabric.

–	–	S	–	S	–	S	–	–
I	I	S	I	S	I	S	I	I
–	S	–	S	–	S	–	S	–
I	S	I	S	I	S	I	S	I
–	–	S	–	S	–	S	–	–
I	I	S	I	S	I	S	I	I
–	S	–	S	–	S	–	S	–
I	S	I	S	I	S	I	S	I

3 SLIP-TWEED STITCH
>< △ [ ]

Multiple of 2 sts, + 1 extra
row 1 (wrong side): col A, P1, * K1, P1; rep from * to end
row 2: col B K1 * S1, K1, rep from * to end
row 3: col B K1 * P1, K1, rep from * to end
row 4: col A K2, S1, * K1, S1; rep from * to last 2 sts, K2.
rep these 4 rows
Different effects can be achieved by altering the order of the colours.
This stitch makes a thick, firm fabric, not pulling in as much as slip-moss st, as the slip-sts only occur on alt rows.

I	I	S	I	S	I	S	I	I
–	I	–	I	–	I	–	I	–
I	S	I	S	I	S	I	S	I
I	–	I	–	I	–	I	–	I

4 TWEED STITCH
>< △ [ ] —

Multiple of 2 sts, + 1 extra
row 1: (right side): col A, K1 * yf, S1p yb, K1: rep from * to end
row 2: col A P2 * yb, S1p, yf, P1: rep from * to last st, P1
row 3: col B as row 1
row 4: col B as row 2
rep these 4 rows

This produces a firm, flat st, not as thick as no 3, which will hold its shape well. Because it does not curl, it can be used for strips of fabric, such as knitted ties or belts, and would also be suitable for jackets or skirts.

I	I	S	I	S	I	S	I	I
I	S	I	S	I	S	I	S	I
I	I	S	I	S	I	S	I	I
I	S	I	S	I	S	I	S	I

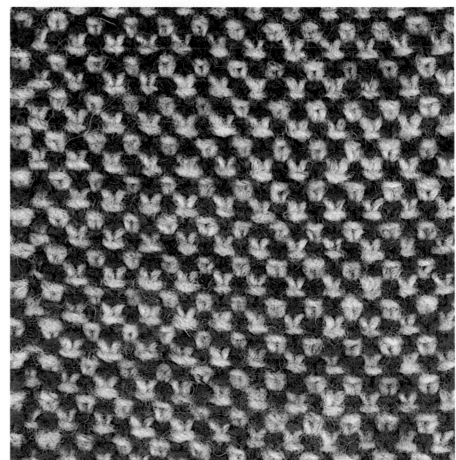

5 3-COLOUR SLIP-STITCH
>< △ [ ]—

Multiple of 6 sts, + 5 extra

Slip all sts p-wise, with yarn on wrong side

foundation row: (wrong side); col A, purl

rows 1 & 2: col B, K1, S3 * K3, S3, rep from * to last st, K1

rows 3 & 4: col C, K4 * S3, K3, rep from * to last st, K1

rows 5 & 6: col A, as rows 1 & 2

rows 7 & 8: col B, as rows 3 & 4

rows 9 & 10: col C, as rows 1 & 2

rows 11 & 12: col A, as rows 3 & 4

Another firm, thick fabric.

–	–	–	–	S	S	S	–	–	–	S	S	S	–	–	–	–
I	I	I	I	S	S	S	I	I	I	S	S	S	I	I	I	I
–	S	S	S	–	–	–	S	S	S	–	–	–	S	S	S	–
I	S	S	S	I	I	I	S	S	S	I	I	I	S	S	S	I
I	I	I	I	I	I	I	I	I	I	I	I	I	I	I	I	I

6 RIBBON STITCH
△

A variation on the above slip-st:

Multiple of 4 sts, + 3 extra

row 1: (right side), col A, K

row 2: col A, P

row 3: col B, K1,.* S1p yab, K3; rep from * to last 2 sts, S1p, K1.

row 4: col B, P1 * S1 yaf, P3, rep from * to last 2 sts, S1, P1

row 5: as row 1

row 6: as row 2

row 7: col C, K3 * S1p yab, K3, rep from * to end

row 8: col C P3 * S1p yaf, P3, rep from * to end

rep these 8 rows, changing colours as desired

This fabric is not as thick as no 5, as it is worked in stocking st, slipping sts for 2 rows only, so does not have the purl rows coming forward to give the extra depth and texture.

I	I	I	I	S	I	I	I	S	I	I	I
I	I	I	I	S	I	I	I	S	I	I	I
I	I	I	I	I	I	I	I	I	I	I	I
I	I	I	I	I	I	I	I	I	I	I	I
I	S	I	I	I	S	I	I	I	S	I	I
I	S	I	I	I	S	I	I	I	S	I	I
I	I	I	I	I	I	I	I	I	I	I	I
I	I	I	I	I	I	I	I	I	I	I	I

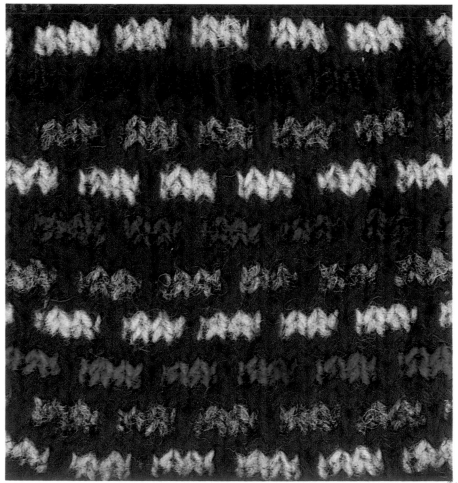

7 SLIP-GARTER & STOCKING ST
△ [ ]

Multiple of 6 sts + 2 extra

row 1: col A, K
row 2: col A, K
row 3: col B, K3 * S2p, yab, K4 * rep to last 3 sts, S2p, K3
row 4: col B, P3 * S2p, yaf, P4 * rep to last 3 sts, S2p, P3
row 5: as row 3
row 6: as row 4
row 7: col A, as row 1
row 8: as row 2

This makes a fairly thick slip-st fabric, as rows 3–6 are pulled up by the slip-sts, and rows 7 & 8, 1 & 2 are garter st, which also pulls up to make thick ridges.

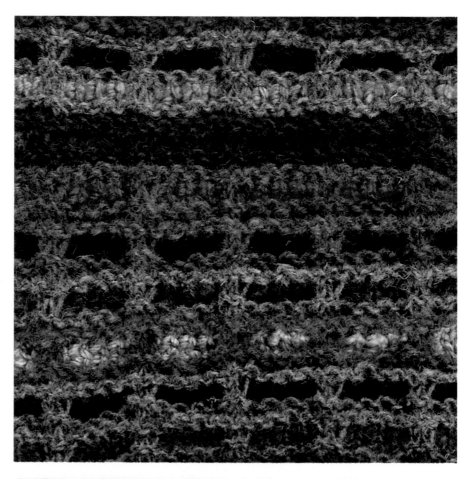

–	–	–	–	–	–	–	–	–	–	–	–	–	–	–	–
I	I	I	I	I	I	I	I	I	I	I	I	I	I	I	I
I	I	I	S	S	I	I	I	I	I	S	S	I	I	I	I
I	I	I	S	S	I	I	I	I	I	S	S	I	I	I	I
I	I	I	S	S	I	I	I	I	I	S	S	I	I	I	I
I	I	I	S	S	I	I	I	I	I	S	S	I	I	I	I
–	–	–	–	–	–	–	–	–	–	–	–	–	–	–	–
I	I	I	I	I	I	I	I	I	I	I	I	I	I	I	I

8 SLIP-STITCH 'WINDOWS'
△ [ ]

Multiple of 8 sts, + 2 edge sts

row 1: col A knit
row 2: col A knit
row 3: col A purl
row 4: col A knit
row 5: col B K1, * S2p, yab, K6, rep from * to last st, K1
row 6: col B P1 * P6, S2p, yaf, rep from *, ending P1.
row 7: as row 5
row 8: as row 6
rep these 8 rows.

The slipped sts come underneath each other, pulling up the length, and making a thick, textured fabric. Variations could be tried with odd nos of sts, staggering the slip-sts in a 'brick' pattern. The 'windows' would then be pulled into a rounder shape.

I	I	I	I	I	I	I	I	S	S	I	I	I	I	I	I	I	I	S	S	I
I	I	I	I	I	I	I	I	S	S	I	I	I	I	I	I	I	I	S	S	I
I	I	I	I	I	I	I	I	S	S	I	I	I	I	I	I	I	I	S	S	I
I	I	I	I	I	I	I	I	S	S	I	I	I	I	I	I	I	I	S	S	I
–	–	–	–	–	–	–	–	–	–	–	–	–	–	–	–	–	–	–	–	–
–	–	–	–	–	–	–	–	–	–	–	–	–	–	–	–	–	–	–	–	–
I	I	I	I	I	I	I	I	I	I	I	I	I	I	I	I	I	I	I	I	I

9 MOSS & SLIP-STITCH
△

Multiple of 8 sts + 2 edge sts
row 1: col A, K
rows 2–12: col A, K1, P1 moss st
row 13: col B, K1 * S2p, yab, K6 * rep to last st, K1
row 14: col B, P1 * P6, S2p, yaf * rep, ending P1
rows 15 & 16 as **13 & 14**
These 16 rows form the pattern
This sample uses variations of col A for the moss st bands, and a contrast range of cols (B) for the slip-st rows (13 & 14).

10 SLIP-STITCH RIDGES
△

In this stitch, the slip-sts sink back, un-like the 'windows' (8) and 'ribbon st' (6) above, where they come forward.
Multiple of 8 sts, + 2 edge sts
row 1: col A, K
row 2: col A, P
row 3: col B, K1 * S2 yab, K6, rep from * to last st, K1
row 4: col B, K1 * K6, S2 yaf, rep from * to last st, K1
rep these 4 rows, and vary by moving the sl-sts along one st every row, to create diagonals.

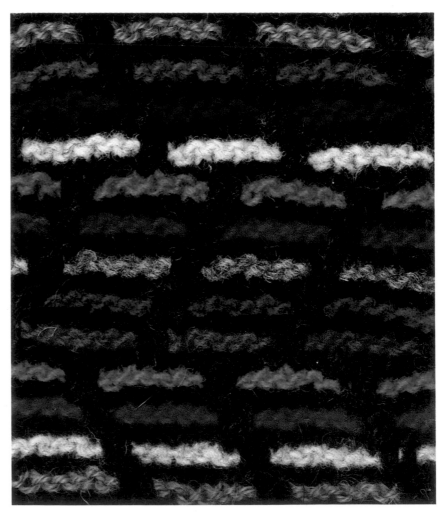

11 RIDGES ON JACQUARD GROUND

△

The ridges are worked as in no 10, on a jacquard-patterned ground in diagonal stripes of 2 sts per colour. Any jacquard pattern could be used as a ground, punctuated with slip-st ridges in any arrangement. Although the fabric grows slowly with so much detailed patterning, this combination of sts gives limitless possibilities for different patterns and textures.

12 RIDGES & TWISTED-STITCH STRIPE

△

Multiple of 12 sts + 2 edge sts
Foundation rows:
1: knit col A
2: purl col A
Pattern:
row 1: col B, K1 * K10, S2 p-wise, yab *
rep to last st, K1
row 2: col B, K1 ' K10, S2 p-wise, yaf ^
rep to last st, K1
row 3: col A, K1 * K10, and work the slipped sts thus: K second st, leaving it on the needle, K first st & slip both off needle * rep to last st, K1
row 4: col A, P
rep these 4 rows
This produces a thick fabric, as the slipped sts pull up.
Twisting the 2 sts in row 3 makes a more prominent vertical stripe.
This sample uses a tie-dyed yarn as the background, col B.

13 SLIP-STITCH RIDGED DIAMONDS ON STRIPED GROUND

△

Multiple of 14 sts + 2 edge sts
Instructions are given for 2 colours, but any number could be used, in order or at random, as in sample.

row 1: col A, K

row 2: col A, P

row 3: (ridges) col B, K1, S2 yab * K10, S4 * rep, ending K10, S2, K1

row 4: slip the same sts as row 1, keeping yaf, and knitting 10 as before

rows 5 & 6 as 1 & 2

row 7: col B, K2 * S2 yab, K8, S2, K2 * rep to end

row 8: slip the same sts as row 7, yaf, and K the K sts

rows 9 & 10 as 1 & 2

row 11: col B, K3 * S2 yab, K6, S2, K4 * rep, ending S2, K3

row 12: slip the same sts as row 11, yaf, and K the K sts

rows 13 & 14 as 1 & 2

row 15: col B, K4 * S2 yab, K4, S2, K6 * rep, ending S2, K4

row 16: slip the same sts as row 15, yaf, and K the K sts

rows 17 & 18 as 1 & 2

row 19: col B, K5 * S2 yab, K2, S2, K8 * rep, ending K5

row 20: slip the same sts as row 19, yaf, and K the K sts

rows 21 & 22 as 1 & 2

row 23: col B, K6 * S4 yab, K10 * rep, ending S4, K6

row 24: slip the same sts as row 23, yaf, and K the K sts

rows 25 & 26 as 1 & 2

row 27: as row 19

row 28: as row 20

Cont in this way, shaping the diamonds by working the pattern backwards, with rows 31 & 32 as rows 15 & 16, etc.

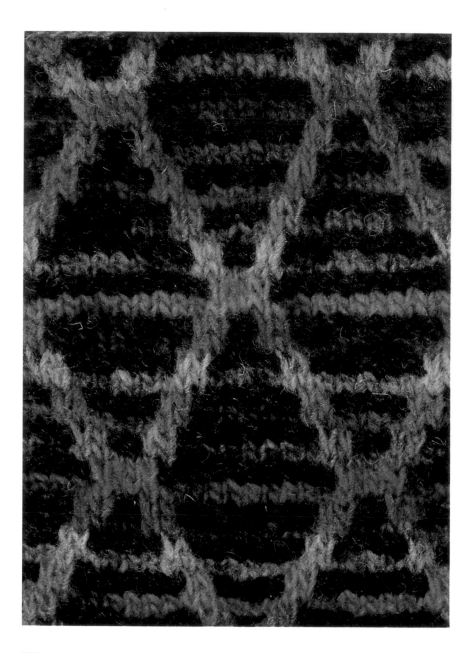

14 SLIP-STITCH WINDOWS WITH BOBBLES
△ [ ]

Multiple of 7 sts, + 2 edge sts
Always keep yarn on wrong side when slipping sts
Moss st (K1, P1) for 4 rows in col A
Change to col B:
** row 1: K1 * K5, S2p * rep to last st, K1
row 2: K1 * S2p, P5 * rep to last st, K1
row 3: as 1
row 4: as 2
row 5: col A, knit
row 6: moss st (K1, P1) until above the first of each pair of sl-sts, and make bobble:
Using a contrast col if preferred, K into the front, back, front, back, and front of the st * turn. K5, turn, P5 * rep * to *.
To finish bobble, lift 2nd st over 1st, then 3rd over 1st, then 4th, then 5th, until only 1st st is left on needle.
Cont moss st for 6 sts, then rep bobble.
row 7: moss st
row 8: moss st 1 more row, then work from **
In this sample, the slip sts and bobbles are placed above each other for the first part, and staggered for the second part.

◁ A

15 BRAMBLE STITCH
A: >< [ ]
B: >< [ ] —

Multiple of 4, + 2 edge sts
row 1: (right side) purl
row 2: K1 * (K1, P1, K1) into next st, P3 tog; rep from * to last st, K1
row 3: P
row 4: K1 * P3 tog, (K1, P1, K1) into next st; rep from * to last st, K1
rep these 4 rows
Sample a) shows 2-row stripes, changing colour on wrong-side rows.
Sample b) shows a jacquard version in 2 colours, changing col for each cluster of 3 sts.

◁ B

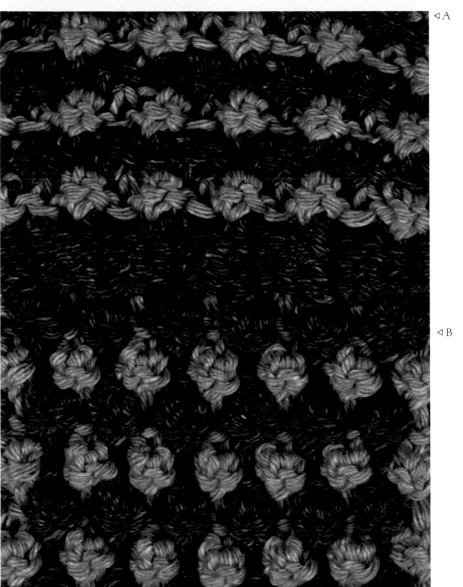

16 EMBOSSED LEAF
[ ]

Multiple of 4 sts + 3 extra

If 2 colours are used, strand the cols on the back, to help the 'leaf' bulge forward.

row 1: P3 col A * K1 col B, P3 col A * rep from * to *

row 2: K3 col A * P1 col B, K3 col A * rep from * to *

row 3: P3 col A * O, K1, O, col B, P3 col A * rep from * to *

row 4: K3 col A * P3 col B, K3 col A * rep from * to *

row 5: P3 col A * O, K3, O, col B; P3 col A * rep from * to *

row 6: K3 col A * P5 col B, K3 col A * rep from * to *

row 7: P3 col A * O, K5, O col B; P3 col A * rep from * to *

row 8: K3 col A * P7 col B, K3 col A * rep from * to *

row 9: P3 col A * S1, K1, psso, K3, K2 tog col B; P3 col A * rep from * to *

row 10: as row 6

row 11: P3 col A * S1, K1, psso, K1, K2 tog col B; P3 col A * rep from * to *

row 12: as row 4

row 13: P3 col A * S1, K2 tog, psso col B; P3 col A * rep from * to *

row 14: as row 2

K 2 rows col A

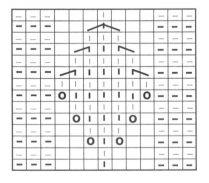

17 OVAL CLUSTERS
[ ]

These are similar to bobbles, but are worked knit-side out, and the way they are started makes a smoother join.

In this sample, the clusters are worked on a purl ground, a knit ground, and a double moss st ground, in contrast colour.

Work to the st where the cluster is to be placed:

row 1: O, K1, O, K1, O, K1; all into 1 st, turn

row 2: P these 6 sts, turn

row 3: S1, K5, turn

row 4: S1, P5, turn

row 5: S1, K5, turn

row 6: P2 tog 3 times, turn

row 7: S1, K2 tog, psso

Continue background

108

18 SINGLE PURL STRIPES

~

Any no of sts
row 1: col A, K
row 2: col A, P
rep for **rows 3 & 4**
row 5: col A, K
row 6: col B, K
This gives a subtle, broken stripe in a purl 'ridge' on a stocking-stitch ground.

19 'RIDGE' STRIPE

~

Worked as no 18, but change colour for rows 5 & 6, to make a more solid ridged stripe.

20 'PICOT' STRIPE

Worked as no 19, except for:
row 6: col B, K2 tog, O, rep to end
This gives a textured ridge which can be used as a decorative stripe, or can be folded to make a picot edge.

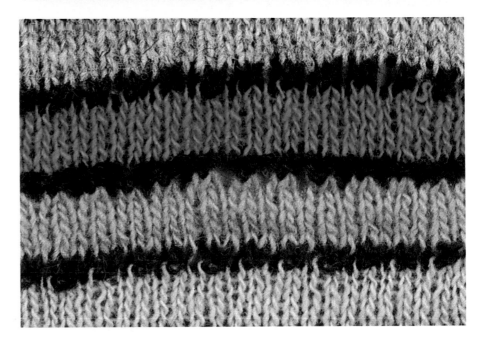

21 WELTING
△ [ ] ~

Any no of sts
row 1: col A, K
row 2: col A, P
row 3: col B, K
row 4: col B, K
row 5: col B, P
row 6: col B, K
rep

This st can be used sideways as a welt, as it forms an elastic st like ribbing, but gives the opportunity to vary the colour in every rib (or welt). It can also be doubled back successfully to make a thicker edging.

22 1 + 1 RIBBING
>< ~

Even no of sts
Every row, K1, P1

For 2-colour rib, use 1 col for K, and 1 for purl on row 1, keeping the colours in the same sts on subsequent rows to make vertical stripes, and the yarn always carried on the wrong side of the fabric.

The horizontal stretch of ribbing is lost in 2-colour rib, which makes a flat fabric with the purl sts more prominent, rather than the knit coming forward and the purl receding.

23 2 + 2 RIB
>< ~

Multiple of 4 sts
K2, P2 every row

a) For 2-colour rib, work as above, beginning K2 col A, P2 col B, keeping
   the colours in vertical stripes.
b) For a 2-colour reversible, stretchy
   rib:
   row 1: both yarns back, K1 A, K1 A
   weaving in B. Both yarns forward,
   P1 B, P1 B weaving in A; rep
   row 2: as row 1 but keep colours in
   vertical stripes

This forms a stretchy rib, different on
each side:
side 1 = col A on knit, mixed A & B on
purl
side 2 = col B on knit, mixed A & B on
purl
This reversible 2-colour effect does not
work for K1, P1 rib, because it is not
possible to weave in when there is only
1 st in each col, and a double (tubular)
fabric results, with col A one side and B
the other (see sample no 36). The same
will happen in K2, P2 rib if the yarns are
not woven in on alt sts.

24 REVERSIBLE FANCY RIB
>< ~

Multiple of 4 sts + 3 extra
Work as follows, with both yarns back
for knit, weaving in on 2nd st, and both
yarns forward for purl, weaving in on
2nd st: the uneven no of sts causes the
pattern to differ from plain ribbing.
row 1: * col A K2, col B P2 * rep to last 3
sts, K2A, P1B
row 2: * col B K2, col A P2 * rep to last 3
sts, K2B, P1A
rep these 2 rows

25 DIAGONAL RIB

>< ~

Multiple of 4 sts
row 1: K2, P2, rep to end
row 2: K2, P2, rep to end
row 3: P1, * K2, P2, rep to last st, K1
row 4: K the purls and P the knits
row 5: P2, K2, rep to end
row 6: P2, K2, rep to end
row 7: K1 * P2, K2, rep to last st, P1
row 8: K the purls and P the knits
2-colour diagonal: work as above, with knits in col A, and purls in col B in row 1, and keeping the colours in the same sts on row 2. When the sts shift sideways in rows 3, 5 & 7, always *knit* the first of the purl sts, ie K2 A; K1, P1 B: so that the new colour makes a clean line above the stitch below. On wrong side rows, K2, P2 as usual.

26 DIAGONAL TEXTURE, twisted stocking st and moss stitch in 2 cols

Multiple of 13 sts
row 1: K4b col A, 9-st moss (on right side rows, * P1 B, K1 A * rep 4 times, P1 B) rep to end
row 2: P1b A, * 9-st moss (on wrong side rows, K1 B, P1 A ending K1 B) P4b A, rep, ending P3b A
row 3: K2b A, * 9-st moss, K4b A * rep, ending K2b A
row 4: P3b A, * 9-st moss, P4b A * rep, ending P1b A
row 5: * 9-st moss, K4b A * rep
row 6: K1 B * P4b A, 9-st moss * rep to last 8 sts, moss st
row 7: 7-st moss beg P1 B, * K4b A, 9-st moss * rep to last st, P1 B, K1 A
row 8: 3-st moss, beg K1 B * P4b A, 9-st moss * rep ending 6-st moss
row 9: 5-st moss, beg P1 B * K4b A, 9-st moss * rep, ending 4-st moss
row 10: 5-st moss, beg K1 B * P4b A, 9-st moss * rep ending 4-st moss
row 11: 3-st moss beginning P1 B * K4b A, 9-st moss * rep ending 6-st moss
row 12: 7-st moss beg K1 B * P4b A, 9-st moss * rep ending 2-st moss
row 13: P1 B * K4b A, 9-st moss * rep, ending 8-st moss
row 14: * 9-st moss, P4b A, rep to end
Cont in this manner, moving the patterns across 1 st per row.

27 DIAGONAL JACQUARD

Worked in stocking st, with 2 sts in one colour, and 4 sts in contrast colours which change every few rows.

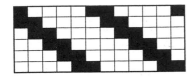

28 DIAGONAL TWISTED RIB

>< ~

Multiple of 8 sts

row 1: col A K4b, P4, rep

row 2: col A K4, P4b, rep

row 3: col B P1 * K4b, P4 * rep ending P3

row 4: col B K3, P4b * K4, P4b * rep to last st, K1

row 5: col A P2 * K4b, P4 * rep ending P2

row 6: col A K2, P4b * K4, P4b * rep, ending K2

row 7: col B P3 * K4b, P4 * rep ending K4b, P1

row 8: col B K1, P4b * K4, P4b * rep ending K3

row 9: col A P4, K4b to end

row 10: col A P4b, K4 to end

row 11: col B K1b * P4, K4b * rep ending K3b

row 12: col B P3b * K4, P4b * rep ending P1b

row 13: col A K2b * P4, K4b * rep ending K2b

row 14: col A P2b * K4, P4b * rep ending P2b

row 15: col B K3b * P4, K4b * rep ending K1b

row 16: col B P1b * K4, P4b * rep ending P3b

Depending on the yarn used, this can make a springy rib (which has been used in the past for bedsocks, as the spiral nature of the fabric prevents the socks from slipping off!), or it can be used decoratively as a diagonal texture.

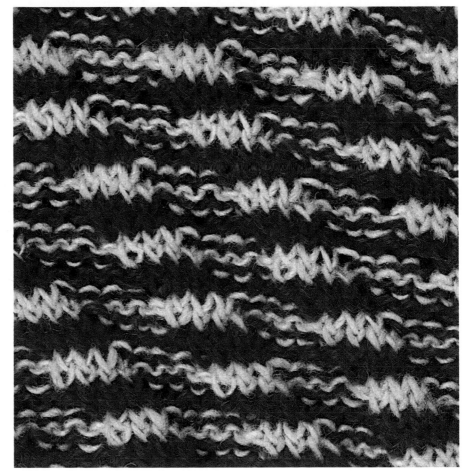

29 PLEATS

>< ~

This pattern produces a pleated fabric if worked in a plain colour, as the knit and purl sts buckle the knitting like ribbing when they come vertically next to each other. If worked in a jacquard pattern, a flat fabric with a pattern of triangles will result, unless the purl sts have the yarn carried on the right side as illustrated in the sample, so that once again the knit stitches come forward, and the purl recedes.

Note: if using 2 colours, use one for all knit sts, and the other for purl, weaving in alternate sts. The finished knitting will have a different effect on each side: one will be col A + mixed A & B, the other will have col B + mixed A & B.

Multiple of 10 sts

row 1: * K2, P2, K6 * rep
row 2: * P5, K3, P2 * rep
row 3: * K2, P4, K4 * rep
row 4: * P3, K5, P2 * rep
row 5: * K2, P6, K2 * rep
row 6: * P1, K7, P2 * rep
row 7: * K2, P8 * rep
row 8: * P1, K7, P2 * rep
row 9: * K2, P6, K2 * rep
row 10: * P3, K5, P2 * rep
row 11: * K2, P4, K4 * rep
row 12: * P5, K3, P2 * rep

30 ZIG-ZAG TEXTURES

Multiple of 8 sts + 1 edge st
cols A, B & C
row 1: K1 A, P1 B all across, ending K1 A
row 2: P2 A * (K1 B, P1 A) x 2, K1 B, P3 A * rep, ending P2 A
row 3: K3 A * P1 B, K1 A, P1 B, K5 A * rep, ending K3 A
row 4: P4 A * K1 B, P7 A * rep, ending P4 A
row 5: P1 C * K7 A, P1 C * rep
row 6: P1 A, K1 C * P5 A, K1 C, P1 A, K1 C * rep ending K1 C, P1 A
row 7: P1 C, K1 A, P1 C, K3 A (P1 C, K1 A) x 2, P1 C, K3 A * rep, ending P1 C
row 8: P1 A, K1 C all across

Cont in this way, bringing in new colours if desired

This is another useful way of making a third shade with 2 colours: each colour can be used 'plain' in the stocking stitch areas, and the two are mixed in the moss st. The moss stitch will look different according to which colour is used for the purl, which pushes forward the colour in the stitch below.

114

31 FEATHER AND FAN
(Sometimes called Old Shale)

O /

Multiple of 11 sts
row 1: * K 2 tog, K2 tog, O, K1, O, K1, O, K2 tog, K2 tog * rep
row 2: purl
row 3: knit
row 4: knit
These 4 rows form the pattern, which can easily be varied from the groups of 4 increases and decreases, by using more or less sts in each group.
In this sample, rows 1 & 2 are worked in grey, and 3 & 4 in black.

32 HERRINGBONE

/

Multiple of 7, + 1 edge st
row 1: (wrong side), purl
row 2: * K2 tog, K2, K1 into back of st below next st on LH needle, K next st, K2 * rep to last st, K1
row 3: purl
row 4: K1, * K2, K into back of next st below, K next st, K2 more, K2 tog, rep from * to end
Knitting into the back of the st below gives a very neat, smooth increase, with no holes or bars. If coloured stripes are knitted across for 1 or 2 rows, a wiggly line is produced, but the zig-zag is less pronounced than in stitches using a double increase and decrease (see no 33).
b) Worked in 2 colours to make vertical stripes: knit the decrease and next 2 sts in col A, and the increase and following 2 sts col B. Repeat the colours on the same sts in rows 2 & 4.

◁A

◁B

115

33 ZIG-ZAGS

Multiple of 10, + 1 edge st
row 1: K1 * O, K3, S2, K1, p2sso, (+)
K3, O, K1 *, rep to end
row 2: purl
These 2 rows form the pattern. For the
stripes, work 2 rows in a contrast colour, the 2nd being knitted instead of
purled.
b) Worked in 2 colours (jacquard), use
col A for sts up to (+), then col B up to
*, and purl the same sts in same colours
on even rows.

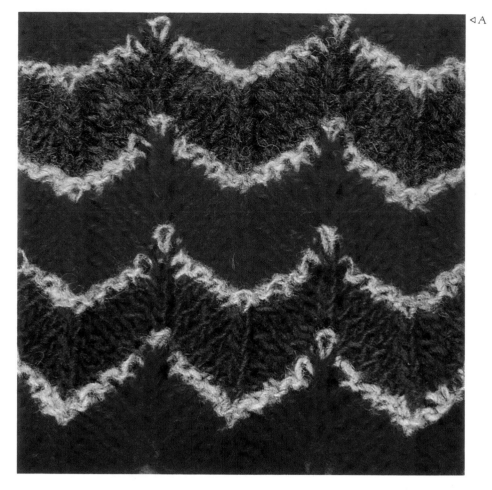

◁A

◁B

34 FALLING LEAF

A: O
B: /

a) Multiple of 10 sts, +1

row 1: K1, * O, K3, S1, K2 tog, psso, K3, O, K1 *, rep * to *

row 2: and all even rows, purl

row 3: K1, * K1, O, K2, S1, K2tog, psso, K2, O, K2 * rep * to *

row 5: K1, * K2, O, K1, S1, K2tog, psso, K1, O, K3 * rep * to *

row 7: K1, * K3, O, S1, K2tog, psso, O, K4 * rep * to *

for coloured stripe as in sample, K 2 rows contrast colour here

row 9: S1, K1, psso * K3, O, K1, O, K3, S1, K2tog, psso *, rep * to last 2 sts, ending S1, K1, psso

row 11: S1, K1, psso * K2, O, K3, O, K2, S1, K2 tog, psso * rep to last 2 sts, S1, K1, psso

row 13: S1, K1, psso * K1, O, K5, O, K1, S1, K2 tog, psso * rep * to *, ending S1, K1, psso

row 15: S1, K1, psso * O, K7, O, S1, K2 tog, psso* rep * to * ending S1, K1, psso

row 16: purl

for coloured stripe, K 2 rows here, with no shaping

b) 2-colour falling leaf:

Use one colour for the increasing sts, and the other for the decreasing group, ie: in row 1, the 'O, K1, O' is in colour A, and the 'K3, S1, K1, psso, K3' in colour B, repeating the colours in the purl rows.

row 3 will be 'O, K3, O' in col A, etc

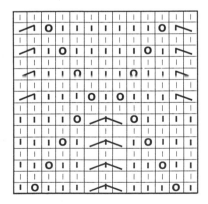

◁ A

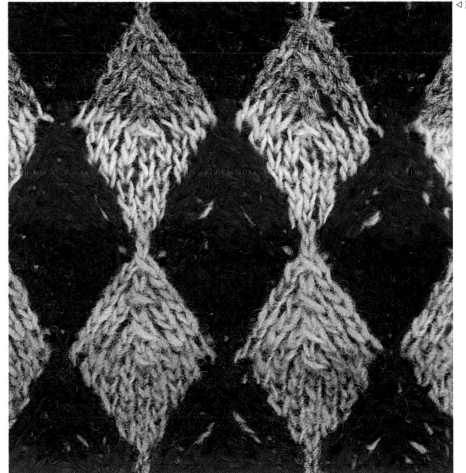

◁ B

35 SCROLL STITCH

A: / B: /

Multiple of 10 sts + 2 edge sts

row 1: (right side) K1 * O, K8, K2tog* K1

row 2: P1 * P2 tog, P7, O, P1* P1

row 3: K1 * K2, O, K6, K2 tog* K1

row 4: P1 * P2 tog, P5, O, P3 * P1

row 5: K1 * K4, O, K4, K2 tog * K1

row 6: P1 * P2 tog, P3, O, P5 * P1

row 7: K1 * K6, O, K2, K2tog * K1

row 8: P1 * P2 tog, P1, O, P7 * P1

row 9: K1 * K8, O, K2 tog * K1

row 10: P1 * O, P8, P2 tog b (thro back of loops) * P1

row 11: K1 * S1, K1, psso, K7, O, K1 * K1

row 12: P1 * P2, O, P6, P2 tog b * P1

row 13: K1 * S1, K1, psso, K5, O, K3 * K1

row 14: P1 * P4, O, P4, P2 tog b * P1

row 15: K1 * S1, K1, psso, K3, O, K5 * K1

row 16: P1 * P6, O, P2, P2 tog b * P1

row 17: K1 * S1, K1, psso, K1, O, K7 * K1

row 18: P1 * P8, O, P2 tog b * P1

rep

In the sample (a), rows 5 & 6 and 14 & 15 are in a contrast colour, showing how the rows are distorted by this pattern, producing a lively, undulating stripe.

In sample (b) p119, different colours are used for each group of stitches: one being the increasing group, and the other the decreasing. The 'O' begins the new colour at the beginning of each new pattern, ie:

row 1: 'O' in col A; and K8, K2 tog col B

row 2: 'O, P1' col A, and continue doing the 'O' and increased sts in this colour, until row 9.

row 10: the 'O' and all subsequent increased sts will be in the new colour.

◁A

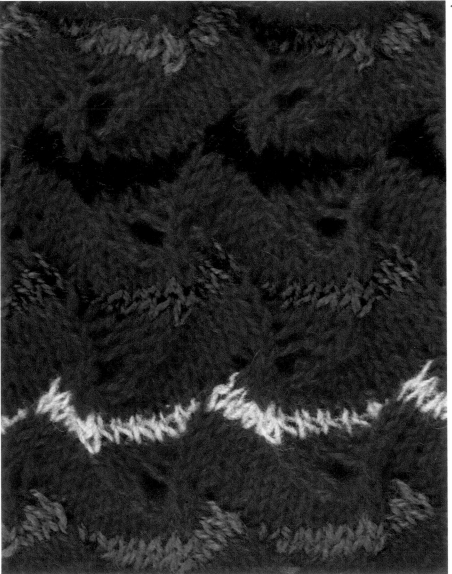

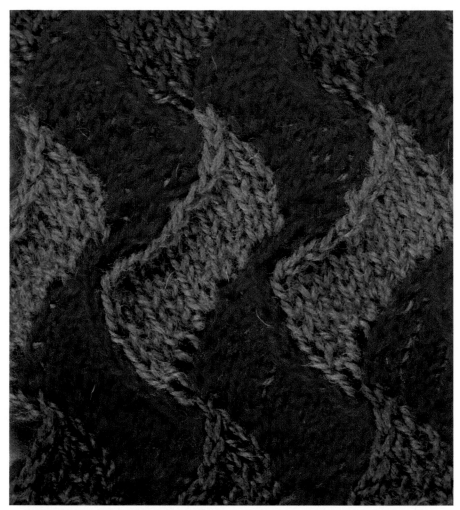

◁ B

36 TUBULAR OR DOUBLE KNITTING
— [ ]

Giving a reversible stocking st in 2 colours.

Note: this st must be worked on circular or double-ended needles back and forth, as the work is not turned at the end of rows 1 & 3.

Cast on an even no of sts

row 1: col A, * K1, yf, S1, yb* rep to end. Don't turn, but slide sts back, and work in the same direction again

row 2: col B * yb, S1, yf, P1 * rep to end. Turn, making sure to cross yarns over each other (this closes the edges of the fabric which will otherwise have a separate front and back)

row 3: col B as row 1

row 4: col A as row 2

rep these 4 rows

This gives a plain stocking st double fabric.

In order to introduce the back colour to the front in blocks or other patterns, proceed as in this sample:

row 1: col A K1, yf, S1, yb, rep for as long as required: for block showing col B, keep using col A: yf, S1, yb, P1, rep for length of block, then change back to first part of row. Don't turn

row 2: col B, yb, S1, yf P1, rep for first part. For block: yb, K1, yf, S1, rep; and back to first part for rest of row

row 3: col B as row 1

row 4: col A as row 2

Once this stitch is mastered, reversible colour designs can be developed, producing geometric or random shapes. Very clear colour contrasts can be used, with no problems of stranding or weaving in, as the 2nd yarn is working a reverse design on the back. It is slow to knit because of the double thickness, and of course the width will be of half the no of sts.

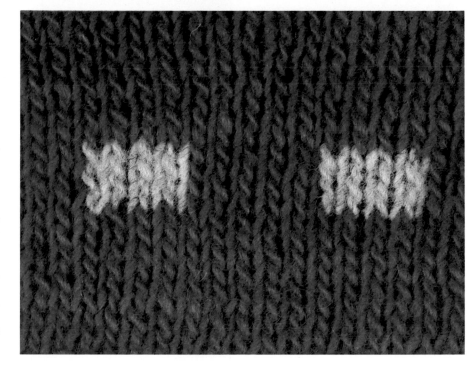

S	I	S	I	S	I	S	I	WS
–	S	–	S	–	S	–	S	WS
–	S	–	S	–	S	–	S	RS
S	I	S	I	S	I	S	I	RS

37 ENTRELACS
/ < >

This stitch is great fun to knit, and not as complicated as it first appears. It is ideal for knitting in the round as there are no straight edges, so side triangles are not necessary: these are only needed for flat pieces. However, base triangles have to be made to start with, and top triangles to finish off – though it all becomes logical once you begin to understand the structure! This is a stitch that has to be tried in order to see how it works, rather than explained.

In sample (a), 4 sts are used for each block, so a multiple of 4 sts is cast on.

1) Base triangles
* K1, turn, P1, turn
S1, K1, turn, S1, P1, turn
S1, K2, turn, S1, P2, turn
S1, K3*
Don't turn; the first group is now complete. Leave these 4 sts on the needle, and carry on with the next st, repeating from * to *. Continue all along the row.

2) First side triangle:
P into front & back of 1st st, turn, S1, K1, turn
Inc into 1st st, P2 tog, (with 1st st of next triangle), turn, S1, K2, turn
Inc in 1st st, P1, P2 tog
Now to continue along row, begin first complete 'block':

3) Purl blocks:
* Pick up and P 4 sts along the side of the next base triangle: the first st is already on the needle, and there should be loops made by the slipped sts at the edge of the base triangle to pick up. Turn.
S1, K3, turn; S1, P2, P2tog (= last st + 1st st of next triangle), turn
rep from * until all sts are joined with next triangle, ending on the purl side
Go on to next block, picking up 4 sts down side of next triangle, as before
Work blocks until the last base triangle remains, then make as follows:

4) Last side triangle:
Pick up and P 4 sts as before, but on every K row, K the 1st 2sts tog. When 1 st is left, this will become the 1st st of next K row of blocks.

5) Knit blocks: Knit side facing
Pick up and K 4 sts down side of block, turn. S1, P3, turn.
S1, K2, K 2 tog thro back of loops (with 1st st of next block), turn. Cont in this way until block is complete, then work along row.

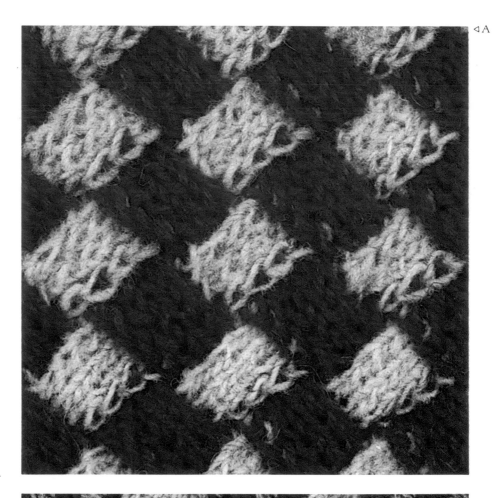

◁ A

◁ B

◁C

Rows of blocks are worked for as long as desired, then the fabric is finished off with

6) the top triangles: knit side facing:
Pick up and K 4 sts as usual. Turn
S1, P3, turn. K2 tog, K2 tog thro backs, turn
S1, P1, turn, K2 tog thro backs. Cont with next top triangle.

The blocks in this fascinating stitch can be of any no of sts, see samples. A 'bias' fabric is produced, which hangs well and has good stretching and draping qualities, so is very comfortable to wear. Pattern and colour can be introduced in endless combinations, from simple textures and stripes to jacquards.

Tension has to be worked out carefully for a garment to be the correct size, as the width is much greater than it would be on the same number of stitches in straight knitting. Shaping is a problem, and the stitch is best used for rectangular or tubular shaped garments, with welts and cuffs providing the styling and firm edges, and possibly 'straight' stitches used for some areas.

38 WOVEN CABLE
>< △ [ ] / I

Multiple of 4 sts
To cable:
a) C4 front or back: slip next 2 sts onto a cable needle and hold at back or front of work, knit next 2 sts from LH needle using B, then knit sts from cable needle using A.
row 1: K2 A, K2 B, rep to end
row 2: P2 B, P2 A, rep
Pattern:
row 1: * C4 front, rep from * to end
row 2: P2 A, P2 B, rep to end
row 3: K2 A * C1 back, rep from * to last 2 sts, K2 B
row 4: P2 B, P2 A, rep to end
b) A much simpler way to work this stitch in 2 colours is to use one colour at a time, changing every 2 rows. The result is very similar to a), with slightly less clarity in the cross-over effect, and a little more stretch; although in both cases the fabric is very thick and firm.

Visually, woven cables are similar to no 37a), where entrelacs are worked on small scale; however, in character they are very different, as the all-over cabling pulls in the stitches to make a firm, thick fabric.

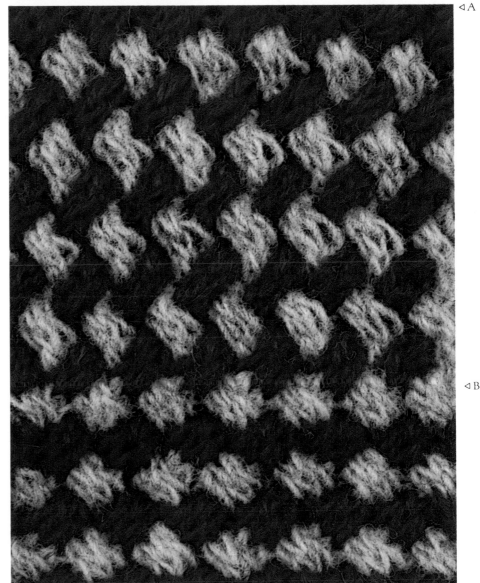

◁A

◁B

121

39 BELL STITCH
[ ] <>

This stitch is worked upwards, and downwards
Multiple of 6 sts, + 5 extra
The sample illustrated begins with moss st, then changes col for a K-2-rows ridge.

a) BELL:

row 1: new colour: * K4, inc in next st by knitting into front and back of st *, rep from * to last 5 sts, K5

row 2: K5 * P1, K5, rep from * to end

row 3: P5 * M1 (by picking up the bar before the next st and knitting it), K1, M1, P5, rep to end

row 4: K5 * P3, K5, rep to end

row 5: P5 * M1, K3, M1, P5, rep to end

row 6: K5 * P5, K5, rep to end

row 7: P5 * M1, K5, M1, P5 rep to end

row 8: K5 * P7, K5, rep to end

row 9: P5 * M1, K7, M1, P5 rep to end

row 10: K5 * P9, K5, rep to end

row 11: change col P5 * cast off 9, P5, rep to end

row 12: K across, so that groups of sts are joined tog, and bells are formed
Between the bells: change colour, knit 1 row, then moss st 5 rows

b) SECOND BELL:

row 1: new colour: K5, * cast on 9 sts by single thumb-twist cast-on (chapter 3 p39), K5, rep to end

row 2: rt side: K across row: this may be slow, as the cast-on sts are usually tight

row 3: change col, K across row

row 4: P5 * S1, K1, psso, K5, K2 tog, P5, rep to end

row 5: K5 * P7, K5, rep to end

row 6: P5 * S1, K1, psso, K3, K2 tog, P5, rep to end

row 7: K5 * P5, K5, rep to end

row 8: P5 * S1, K1, psso, K1, K2 tog, P5, rep to end

row 9: K5 * P3, K5, rep to end

row 10: P5 * S1, K2 tog, psso, P5, rep to end

row 11: K5 * P1, K5, rep to end

row 12: P5 * K2 tog, P4, rep to end

◁ A

◁ B

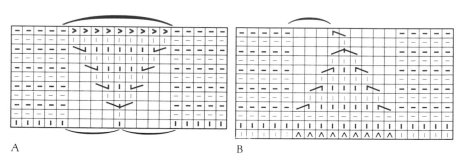

A   B

40 BELL-FRILL EDGE
<> ~

For a frill at the top edge of the fabric, work as for the first part of no 39, casting off all sts on row 11.

For a frill at the bottom edge, follow instructions for the second part of no 39, casting on sts as in row 1, allowing a multiple of 14 + 5 edge sts: 9 for each frill with 5 plain sts between. (Adjust the no of sts for different sized frills.)

41 GORES
<> ~

a) The striped sample shown is worked as for the first part of no 39, but only increasing every 8th row instead of alternate rows, with 2 rows of each colour.

b) The jacquard sample is shaped as in the second part of no 39, decreasing every 6th row, and the pattern is worked with yarns woven at the back of the knit sections, and at the front of the purl sections.

◁ A

◁ B

42 TRIANGLE
/ O

This begins at the centre of the long side;

cast on 7 sts

row 1: (wrong side) purl

row 2: K2, O, K1, O, K1 (centre), O, K1, O, K2

row 3: and all wrong-side rows, purl

row 4: K2, O, K3, O, K1, O, K3, O, K2

row 6: K2, O, K5, O, K1, O, K5, O, K2

Cont in this way, with a K2 border at each side. Inc next to each border, and either side of centre st, until there are 15 sts each side of centre st.

K 2 rows in contrast col to make a ridge.

Lacey pattern:

row 10: change col, K2, O, K1, * O, K2 tog * rep * to * to centre st: O, K1, O: * S1, K1, psso, O, * rep * to * until 3 sts left, K1, O, K2

row 11: P

row 12: K2, O, K2 * O, K2 tog * rep * to * until 1 st before centre, K1, O, K1, O, K1, * S1, K1, psso, O * rep * to * to last 4 sts, K2, O, K2

row 13: P

Rep these 4 rows until there are 12 rows of this pattern.

K2 rows in contrast col to make a ridge

Plain st st band:

row 1: change col, K2, O, K to centre st, O, K1, O, K to last 2 sts, O, K2

row: purl. Rep these 2 rows.

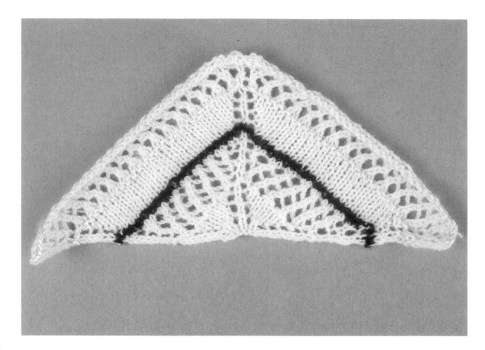

43 TEXTURED CHEVRON STITCH
>< /

Multiple of 8 sts

Border:

row 1: purl

row 2: knit

row 3: P

row 4: K

Pattern: change col

row 1: * K2, M1 (by picking up and knitting the bar bet sts in row below), S1, K1, psso * rep to centre of row

Change pattern: * K2 tog, M1, K2 * rep to end

row 2: purl

row 3: as row 1

row 4: as row 2

row 5: change col, as row 1

row 6: knit

Either half of this pattern could be used alone to make a bias fabric slanting to the left or right.

WS Border

44 HEXAGONAL MEDALLION

Beginning in the centre, working with a set of 4 double-ended needles, and transferring to a circular needle when there are enough sts.

Using 2 of the double-ended needles, cast on 6 sts.

round 1: O, K1, O, K1 onto needle 1
      rep onto needle 2
      rep onto needle 3

round 2: joining into a circle by beginning again at needle 1, knit the 4 sts on each needle

round 3: change col, O, K2, O, K2 on each needle

round 4: and all even rounds, knit

round 5: change col, O, K3, O, K3 on each needle

Continue in this way, increasing at the beginning and middle of each needle on odd rounds, and knitting even rounds.

45 OCTAGONAL MEDALLION

Worked as for no 44, using 5 double-ended needles; holding the sts on 4 and knitting on the 5th. If it is difficult to obtain a set of 5, a short circular needle of the correct size could be used as the 5th.

The increases are worked as in no 44, at the beg and middle of each needle, making 8 incs in each alternate round. Apart from the visual difference of the 8 increases as compared with the 6 in no 44, the greater no of sts increased will make a flat or even slightly rippled piece of knitting, whereas no 44 will be just flat, or slightly domed: but this will depend on the kind of st being used; ie jacquard patterns are inclined to pull in so that the increases will take effect more slowly, so if a flat piece of fabric is planned, 8 or more increases per round should be used.

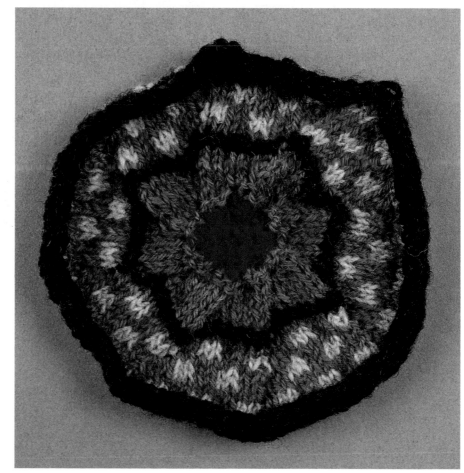

46 JACQUARD GRID

Multiple of 6 sts
Yarns carried at back of work.

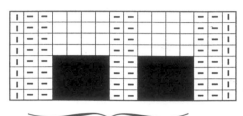

repeat

47 STRETCHY CABLE
>< ~

Multiple of 8 sts
Yarns woven at back for knit sts, and at
front for purl sts.

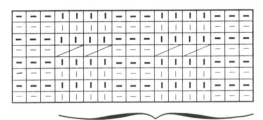

repeat

48 JACQUARD SQUARES

Multiple of 10
Yarns woven at back.

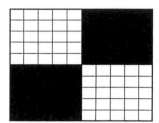

49 JACQUARD TRIANGLES

Multiple of 6
Yarns woven at back.

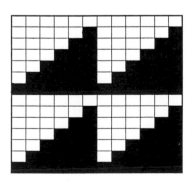

50 JACQUARD ZIG-ZAG & RIDGES

Multiple of 10
Yarns woven at back.

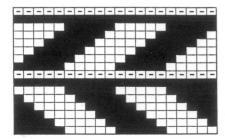

51 JACQUARD DIAMONDS & RIDGES

Multiple of 8
Yarns woven at back.

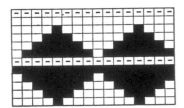

9
PROJECTS

The projects in this chapter begin with simple, flat-shaped designs for shawls, and progress to a basic jumper, then to a more complicated jacket, cushions and hats, all worked in one piece. Written instructions and charts are given for making them as illustrated.

However, they need not necessarily be reproduced as they are, but can be used as starting points for ideas to be developed, extended, expanded or altered; rather like recipes for cooking which vary depending on what ingredients are at hand. Different fibres or yarns could be used; the colours could be changed, with different textures and patterns; or the shapes could be extended and varied, using the guidelines set out in chapter 7.

The shawl and scarf are simple flat shapes, but slightly unusual in construction as they are both 'bias' fabrics, so the knitting is formed at a slant, and will have good draping qualities.

The way the triangular shawl is constructed could be used for a poncho or cape by doubling the shape, with four increase points; for a poncho, beginning with the centre with enough stitches for a head-opening, and knitting in the round; and for a cape, working back and forth with a front opening.

The straight (slanting) shawl could be made larger for an evening wrap, or smaller to become a scarf.

The jumper is a plain, basic shape, as described in chapter 7, relying on the pattern of the fabric for interest. The

straightforward geometric jacquard design used here is given more variety by juggling the colours round; this one has a colour repeat for the sake of writing a chart, but the arrangement of colours could be random. The small flashes of brighter colours lend emphasis to the borders and 'seams' (knitted seams, not sewn).

The jacket is a more complicated shape, still knitted in one piece with only an underarm seam, but in a more fitted style. The stitch used is very simple, with moss stitch stripes on the body, and a slip-stitch for the sleeves, so only one colour is being knitted at a time.

Cushions can be knitted in all sorts of shapes; for this project squares have been used, but with the centre as a starting point rather than the edge. This idea could be developed to make families of cushions using the same colour scheme, with patterns dictated by different constructions: perhaps beginning from a corner and working diagonally, or working a quarter at a time and picking up stitches along the edges of each quarter: a useful way of trying out ideas and using up oddments of colours; or a planned project furnishing a room with coordinating cushions.

Hats: again, a wonderful way to try out ideas for colours and patterns while making something to be worn. Think of them as a sculptural, 3-dimensional shape, and experiment!

SHAWLS

TRIANGULAR SHAWL

MATERIALS

100g 2-ply wool (col B)
100g silk noile (col C)
50g black wool (col A)
50g cream tussah silk (col D)

Circular needles size 3³/₄mm (9)
Straight needles can be used, but it is easier to manage the width on a long circular needle

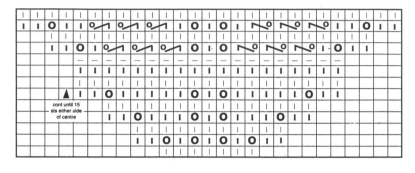

METHOD

Beginning at the centre of the long edge, working back and forth throughout:

Cast on 7 sts col C
row 1: (wrong side) purl
row 2: K2, O, K1, O, K1 (centre), O, K1, O, K2
row 3: and all wrong-side rows, purl
row 4: K2, O, K3, O, K1 (centre), O, K3, O, K2
row 6: K2, O, K5, O, K1, O, K5, O, K2
Cont in this way, keeping K2 at each side as a border, inc 1 st (=O) next to borders, and 1 either side of centre st, until there

are 15 sts altogether each side of centre st. K2 rows col A (no shaping) to make a ridge.
Lacey pattern:
row 10: change to col B. K2, O, K1, * O, K2 tog * rep * to * to centre st: O, K1 (centre), O: * S1, K1, psso, O * rep * to * until 3 sts left: K1, O, K2
row 11: purl
row 12: K2, O, K2 * O, K2 tog *, rep * to * until 1 st before centre, K1, O, K1, O, K1, * S1, K1 psso, O *, rep * to * to last 4 sts, K2, O, K2
row 13: purl
Rep rows 10 to 13 three more times (12 rows of this pattern altogether)
K 2 rows col A to make a ridge

Plain st st band:
Using col C, K2, O, K to centre st: O, K1, O: K to last 2 sts, O, K2
Wrong-side rows, purl
Work 12 rows of this st st band
Continue alternating the lacey pattern with the plain st st, with ridges col A or D between, until the shawl measures 72cm from centre in a straight line (see diagram for where to measure), finishing on the nearest ridge.
Cast off using the ridge colour, fairly loosely, so the edges do not pull.
Sew in ends.
If the long edge is at all uneven, crochet a single or double crochet edging to make it firm.

Triangular shawl

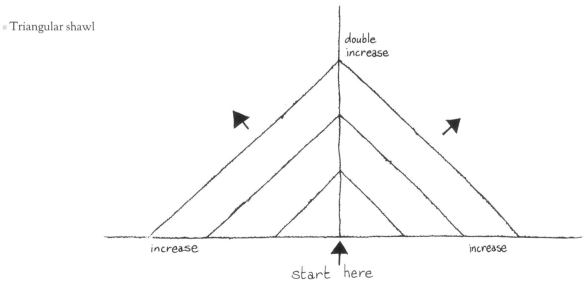

double
increase

increase   increase

start here

DIAGONAL SHAWL

MATERIALS

4-Ply wool col A, 200g
Tussah silk col B 50g

Needles size 3¾mm (9)

Shawls, triangular and diagonal

METHOD

Cast on 101 sts col A
Knit 6 rows to make a garter st border
Begin pattern:
row 1: K2 * O, P2 tog, P2; O, K2 tog, K2
* rep to last 3 sts, O, P2 tog, P1
row 2: K3 * P4, K4, rep to last 2 sts ending P2
Rep these 2 rows for 8 rows altogether, then work 2 rows col B:
1: as row 1
2: P3 * K4, P4, rep to last 2 sts, ending K2.
(This makes a garter st ridge by reversing Ks and Ps.)

Continue working 8 rows pattern col A, with ridges col B between until shawl measures 150cm.
Finish by matching the beginning, with 6 rows garter st col A.

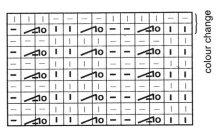

SIMPLE JUMPER

MATERIALS

Munkagarn wool or 4-ply equivalent in 6 colours:
300g col A (navy)
200g col B (mid-blue)
100g each cols C (light blue)
D (grey), E (red), F (orange)

Circular needles size 3¼mm (10) and 3mm (11).

TENSION

26 sts and 31 rows = 10cm over pattern.

MEASUREMENTS

Loose-fitting style, for chest/bust sizes 92cm/36in (99 cm/39in, 107cm/42in).

METHOD

BODY

Using needles size 3mm (11) and col A, cast on 280 (300,320) sts. Work in rib for 7cm:

■ Chart for ribbing

P2 col A, K2 col D, working in the round: change cols for the last 4 rows to A & F: see illustration.
Change to needles size 3¼mm (10), & K 1 round, P 1 round col A to make a ridge.
Begin pattern from chart, and work straight until work measures 34(37,40)cm from beg.

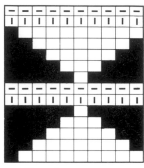

■ Chart for main pattern

Divide for armholes: work on half the sts for back: 140(150,160) sts, putting the front sts on a spare circular needle or holder.
Work straight back and forth for 26cm, to nearest complete pattern, ending cds A and E. Put sts on a spare needle or holder.

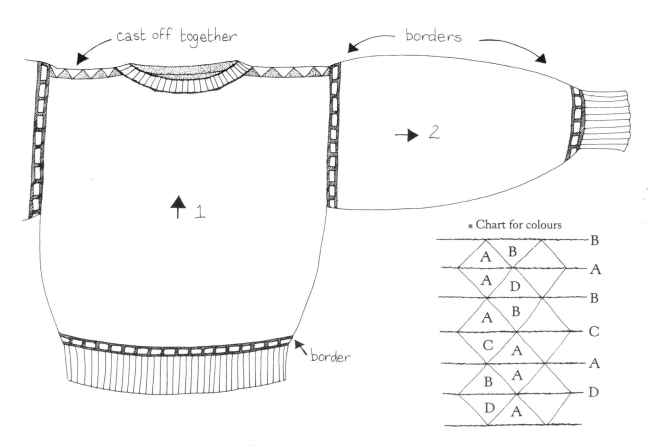

■ Construction of simple jumper

132

FRONT

Work as for back until 20cm from armholes.

NECK

Pattern 51(56,61) sts, pattern 38 sts and leave on a holder, pattern 51(56,60) sts.
Cont in pattern on one side at a time, dec 1 st at neck edge *every* row until 35(40,45) sts remain.
Work straight to match back; then work other side the same.

SHOULDER

Put 35(40,45) sts of front parallel with 35(40,45) sts of corresponding back shoulder, wrong sides tog, and cast off tog using a 3rd needle and working through both back and front, to make a ridge on the outside col A.

SLEEVES

Beginning at base of armhole, right side of work facing, pick up and K 150 sts round armhole, col A. Pick sts up evenly, 75 up front, and 75 down back.
Sleeves may be knitted back and forth, or in the round, going onto a set of 4 double-ended needles when there are too few sts for circular needle.
K 1 row col A to make ridge if working back and forth, *or* purl 1 round col A.
Follow chart for sleeve band pattern, then work straight for 14 rows/rounds.

■ Chart for sleeve band pattern

Dec 1 st at each end of every 4th row (if working in the round, dec 1 each side of imaginary seam underarm) until sleeve measures 40(42,44)cm.

* Adjust sleeve length here: try on to check length *
Change to needles size 3mm (11), and K 2 rows col A, dec evenly along 1st row to make 64 sts.
Work in rib as for welt cols A & F for 4 rows, then A & D until cuff measures 7cm. Cast off col A.

NECK

Using a short circular needle size 3mm(11), right side facing, pick up and K round neck col A:
70 sts from back of neck, 15 sts along side of neck, 38 from front neck holder, and 15 sts along other side of neck. P 1 round col A, then rib as before cols A & D for 2½cm. Cast off (not too tight) col A.

Sew in loose ends, and underarm seam if there is one.

■ Square cardigan with frilled sleeves;
moss and slip-stitch pattern

SQUARE CARDIGAN
WITH FRILLED SLEEVES

MATERIALS

Munkagarn or other 4-ply wool in 5 colours:
200g col A: 4271 (purple)
200g col B: 4262 (burgundy)
200g col C: 4277 (grey)
100g each D: 4317 (gold) and E: 4282 (mustard).

Circular needles size 3mm (11) & 3¼mm (10)

TENSION

22 sts and 40 rows = 10cm over moss st pattern.

MEASUREMENTS

To fit comfortably sizes 97cm (38in), 102cms (40in) and & 107cm (42in)

METHOD

WAISTBAND
Using needles size 3mm(11), cast on 28 sts col C.
row 1: knit
row 2: purl
row 3: change col, knit
row 4: knit
row 5: purl
row 6: knit
Colour sequence: all ridges (rows 3–6) col A, rows 1 & 2 cols C, D, C, E, rep.

■ Chart for ribbing

Rep these 6 rows in col sequence, weaving in loose ends as you go, until there are 58 (60,62) ridges and furrows, casting off on row 2 of pattern.

BODY
Using needles size 3¼mm (10), pick up and knit 262 (276, 290) sts col E evenly along the **untidier** edge of waistband.
Mark with pins the halfway, quarter and eighth points, and pick up approximately an eighth between pins, so that the sts are evenly spread.
K 1 row col E to make a ridge.

Work in pattern (see below) back and forth across the whole width of the jacket until it measures 20 (21, 22)cm from beg, including welt.
Pattern: K1, P1 moss st in 2 rows of each colour in this order: A, C, A, B, rep.

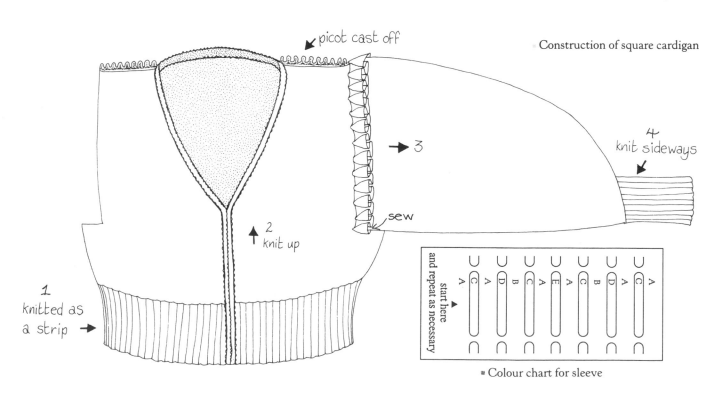

picot cast off

Construction of square cardigan

1 knitted as a strip →

↑ 2 knit up

→ 3

sew

4 knit sideways

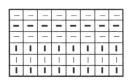

start here and repeat as necessary

■ Colour chart for sleeve

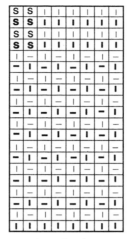

■ Chart for body pattern

Divide for armholes: pattern across 65(69,72) sts of right front, and put these sts on a holder. Pattern across 132(138,146)sts of back, turn, leaving the last 65(69,72) sts on a holder for left front.

BACK
Rejoin wool, cast off 23 sts at beg of next 2 rows. 86(92,100)sts left.
Cont straight in pattern until work measures 26cms from armholes, hold sts.

FRONTS
Cast off 23 sts at armhole edge, 42(46,49) sts left, then work straight at armhole edge, but dec 1 st at front edge on next and every 6th row until there are 21 (25, 28) sts left. Cont straight in pattern until it measures same as back.

SHOULDER
Put the sts of front shoulder parallel with corresponding 21 (25, 28) sts of back shoulder, wrong sides tog, and with col C, cast off both front and back tog in picot:
Using a 3rd needle to knit with, knit thro each front and back st tog as one st: cast off 3 * put right-hand st back onto left-hand needle, cast on 3 (by 'knitting on'), cast off 5 * rep from * to * until all sts cast off.
Note: you might need to use a smaller sized needle for picot cast-off if you are a loose knitter.

SLEEVES
Using needles size 3¼mm (10), and col A, pick up and K 150 sts round armhole (not under arm), see diagram: 75 sts up front, 75 down back. K back 1 row for ridge, col A.
Sleeve is knitted back and forth (on circular needle).
Bell Frill: using col C, K 1 row, P 1 row.
row 1: P3, * K into next st thro front & back, (to make 2 sts), P 5 *, rep * to *ending P3
row 2: K3 * K6, P1 * rep, ending K3
row 3: P3 * O, K 1, O, P6 * rep, ending P3
row 4: K3 * K6, P3 * rep ending K3
row 5: P3 * O, K3, O, P6 * rep, ending P3

■ Chart for sleeve

■ Chart for sleeve frill

row 6: K3 * K6, P5 * rep ending K3
row 7: P3 * O, K5, O, P6 * rep, ending P3
row 8: K3 * K6, P7 * rep, ending K3
row 9: P3 * O, K7,O, P6 * rep, ending P3
row 10: K3 * K6, P9 * rep ending K3
row 11: change to col E
row 12: P3 * cast off the 9 sts of the 'bell' P6 * rep, ending P3
knit col E

Using col A, begin sleeve pattern (see chart for colours): knit 1 row, then moss st (K1, P1) 15 rows. Change col and work slip-st pattern: make sure that the pattern is centred on the sleeve, so that 'K6' comes at centre.
* **row 1:** K6, S2 p-wise, yab, rep to end.
row 2: (matching sl-sts), P6, S2, yaf, rep to end
rep rows 1 & 2.
Change col, K1 row, moss st 15 rows *
See chart for cols; rep * to * throughout sleeve, but after the first band of sl sts, dec 2 sts in middle of every 6th row, thus:
Pattern 73, S1, K1, PSSO, K2 tog; pattern 73.
Keep the decs in the centre of the sleeve, so the next dec will be pattern 72, dec, etc.
Adjust the pattern to fit the decs.

When the sleeve measures 40cm to nearest complete pattern, without stretching (adjust length here to fit) dec evenly along the row to 66 sts.
Change to needles size 3mm (11), K 2 rows col E. cast off (or leave on holder for grafting cuff).

CUFF
Using needles size 3mm (11), cast on 24 sts, and follow waistband pattern for 17 ridges, ending with a ridge. Cast off.

NECK AND BANDS
Using needles size 3mm (11), and col A, pick up sts and knit, beginning at bottom of right front:
28 sts from welt, 23 up straight part of front, 56 along slope of neck, 44(42,44)sts from back of neck, 56 down slope, 53 down front, and 28 from welt.
Note: the band should not pull or pucker: adjust the no of sts if necessary for your tension.
row 2: knit
row 3: purl (the band is reverse st st, purl-side out)
row 4: make buttonholes: knit until end of right neck slope, beginning of straight right front, and make buttonhole: cast off 2 sts, K9. Make 5 buttonholes altogether, with about 9 sts between; leaving 2 sts after the last buttonhole.
row 5: purl, casting on 2 sts over each hole, by twisting 2 sts onto the right-hand needle with the thumb.
row 6: knit
row 7: cast off: be very careful to cast off loosely where the slope of neck begins, and firmly round the back of neck.

TO MAKE UP
Attach cuffs to sleeves, either graft or sew with ladder st: this will make a seam with some 'give': the seam must not be too tight.
Sew sleeve seam from cuff to underarm; see diagram for joining underarm.
Attach buttons.
Press very lightly, if at all, as some of the character of the moss and slip-st can be lost with overpressing.

■ Hats

CUSHIONS

SQUARE CUSHION

MATERIALS

Double knitting wool (or cotton):
100g each of 7 colours.

Needles size 3¾mm (9)
1 circular, and 5 double-ended (if these are difficult to obtain, use a set of 4, with a short circular needle as the 5th). Zip fastener in matching colour, 30cm long.

METHOD

Beginning in the centre, cast on 8 sts col A onto one double-ended needle.
row 1: Knit into the back of sts col A
row 2: * inc into first 2 sts by knitting into front and back of each st *
Using next needle, rep * to * into the next 2 sts
Rep on next 2 needles again, so that at the end of the row, 4 needles are holding 4 sts each.
round 3: join into a round, and knit
round 4: inc into 1st and last st on each needle, by picking up and knitting the loop *before* the first st, and *after* the last st.
round 5: knit
round 6: purl
Now begin pattern from chart, working

the new sts into the pattern, and beginning the pattern for each side of the square anew: ie the pattern will not continue round the corners, where it increases. For the larger patterns, count the sts and place the pattern so it matches on each corner.

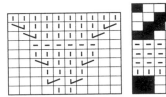

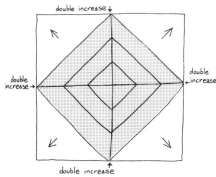

■ Square cushion design: shaded areas are worked first, in the round. As a variation, continue to knit corner sections, decreasing on either edge to make a larger cushion

The increases are made as described in round 4, on 2 out of every 3 rounds, the 3rd being worked without shaping – regardless of whether it is a knit or purl (ridge) round.
As soon as there are enough sts, change to a circular needle.
Continue until it measures 23cm from the centre straight to the edge (not the diagonal), and finishing with a ridge. Work the cushion back either the same, or in another pattern, or plain.

JOINING

If the sts for the two pieces have been cast off, insert the zip:
Place the 2 pieces flat, edge to edge, and tack the zip in place. Sew in firmly (by hand is easier), making sure the knitting is not pulled.
Now join the remaining 3 sides, continuing round the corners to the ends of the zip, either by sewing or crochet.
Alternatively, if the sts are held on 2 circular needles, they can be cast off tog:
Firstly, cast off 1 edge of each piece so the zip can be inserted, then put back and front wrong sides tog, and cast off through both, using a 3rd needle (see diagram p77).

SQUARE CUSHION, SPIRAL PATTERN

MATERIALS

Double knitting wool
a) *Striped cushion*
200g col A, dark brown
oddments of colours for random stripes
b) *Jacquard pattern*
100g each colour
A dark blue
B dark brown
C mid-brown
D mid-grey
E light grey

Needles size 3¾mm (9), 1 circular, and 5 double-ended (if these are difficult to obtain, use a set of 4, with a short circular needle as the 5th).

METHOD

Both cushions: beginning in the centre, cast on 8 sts col A onto one double-ended needle.
row 1: knit into the back of sts col A
row 2: * inc into first 2 sts by knitting into

front and back of each st *
Using next needle, rep * to *
Rep on next 2 needles again, so that at the end of the row, 4 needles are holding 4 sts each
round 3: join into a round, and knit
round 4: inc into 1st on each needle, by picking up and knitting the loop *before* the st
round 5: increase in the same way, knitting round
round 6: increase in the same way, purling round

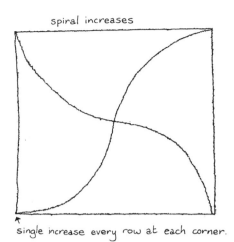

spiral increases

single increase every row at each corner.

■ Square cushion, spiral pattern design

a) *For stripey cushion:* repeat these 4 rounds in stripes of 2 rounds st st (K 2 rounds), and 2 rounds ridge (K1 round, P1 round), in colour sequence: ie all ridges in col A, with random colours between.

b) *jacquard pattern;* follow chart.

The increases are made every round, regardless as to whether it is a knit or purl (ridge) round.

As soon as there are enough sts, change to a circular needle.

Continue until the fabric measures 23cm from the centre straight to the edge (not the diagonal), (a) finishing with a ridge, and (b) the nearest complete pattern.

Make a second piece for the cushion back, and join as for square cushion.

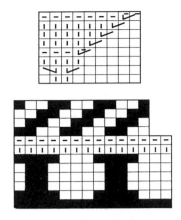

Note: if you are a tight knitter in jacquard patterns, you might need to increase 2 sts each time so that the knitting lies flat.

HATS

MATERIALS

Thick wool or cotton, and rough silk; or any DK yarn, 75g in all. Needles no 9: 4 double-ended, and a short circular (40cm, 50cm or 60cm).

MEASUREMENTS

54cm (21in) circumference.

METHOD

Cast on 6 sts onto one double-ended needle, col A.

round 1: using 2nd needle, * yarn over (O), K1, O, K1*

3rd needle: rep * to *

4th needle: rep * to *

round 2: joining into a circle, K all round

round 3: change to col B, and on each needle, O, K2, O, K2

round 4: *purl* all round.

Continue in stripes of K2 rounds col A, K1 round, P1 round col B, inc at beg and middle of each needle on the first row of each stripe.

Change to the circular needle when there are enough sts.

Cont until there are 120 sts (O, K19); but

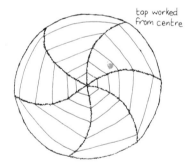

top worked from centre

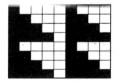

■ Hat structure

knit sides downwards

finishing on a 'ridge'.

Now beg straight sides of hat: follow chart, and work straight in pattern for 8cm or to nearest complete pattern: length can be adjusted here.

To finish: using col B, K 1 round, then P 4 rounds and cast off.

Note: be very careful that this 'rim' is not looser than the patterned part; if it seems to be, then decrease 6 sts in the 1st purl round and cast off firmly to make a neat edge.

To finish: sew in thread at centre, and fasten off loose ends.

The size of the hat can easily be adjusted by making more, or fewer, increases, ie finish crown at 114 sts for a smaller size, or go on to 126 sts for one larger.

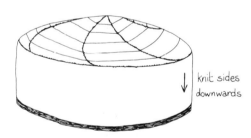

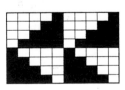

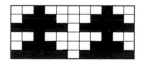

SUPPLIERS

YARNS

The International Wool Secretariat produces a comprehensive list of wool and worsted spinners and suppliers: the address of the UK branch is:
Wool House
Carlton Gardens
London SW1Y 5AE

Useful yarn suppliers include:

British Mohair Spinners Ltd
Midland Mills
Valley Road
Bradford
West Yorkshire, BD1 4RL
(A variety of wools, natural and dyed, and fancy yarns)

Brockwell Wools
Stansfield Mill
Stansfield Mill Lane
Triangle
Sowerby Bridge
West Yorkshire, HX6 3LZ
(Dyed wools and cottons)

Fibrecrafts at Barnhowe
Elterwater
Ambleside
Cumbria LA22 9HW
(A variety of fibres and yarns, natural and dyed, including Swedish linens and Munkagarn wool, as used in Chapter 9 Projects)

William Hall & Co (Monsall) Ltd
177 Stanley Road
Cheadle Hume
Cheshire, SK8 6RF
(Swedish linens and cottons in natural and dyed colours)

Jamieson and Smith Ltd
90 North Road
Lerwick ZE1 0PQ, Shetland Isles
(Shetland and Aran Yarns, including 2-ply shawl wool)

Rowan Yarns
Green Lane Mill
Washpit
Holmfirth
West Yorkshire
(A variety of dyed and fancy yarns, and indigo-dyed cotton)

Texere Yarns
College Mill
Barkerend Road
Bradford
West Yorkshire, BD3 9AQ
(Natural silks and cottons, as well as dyed silk, cottons and wools)

Yeoman Yarns Ltd
31 High Street
Kibworth
Leicester LE8 0HS
(A variety of dyed wools and cottons)

BUTTONS

Buttons seen in the photographs in this book are hand made, and available from

Helen Ablitt
The Old Post Office
East Pennard
Shepton Mallet Somerset BA4 6TU
(Ceramic buttons, plain and embossed)

Chris Baker
Hunters Moon
Gasden Copse
Witley Surrey GU8 5QD
(Wooden toggles in natural wood; the examples in this book have been dyed by the author)

Carole Scott
Rondellerie Cottage
Sark, Channel Islands
(Salt-glazed ceramic buttons, square and round with embossed patterns and colours)

OTHER KNITTING SUPPLIES

Fibrecrafts
Style Cottage
Lower Eashing
Godalming
Surrey GU7 2QD
(Fibres and yarns, natural and chemical dyes and equipment, yarn winders and swifts, specialist textile books and periodicals from around the world)

Spinners
Fakenham Road,
Beetley
Dereham
Norfolk NR20 4BT
(Swifts, ball winders, knitting sheaths, knitting graph paper)

OTHER USEFUL ADDRESSES

Crafts Council
44a Pentonville Road London N19BY
The Crafts Council publish *Crafts* magazine, which advertises suppliers of equipment and materials, and reviews designers' work, exhibitions, and books.

Association of the Guilds of Spinners, Weavers and Dyers: the Crafts Council will supply addresses of local guilds for lectures, demonstrations, workshops and information.

The Knitting and Crochet Guild
Mrs A Budworth, Membership Secretary
228 Chester Road North
Kidderminster
Worcestershire DY10 1TH
A quarterly magazine is published, local groups hold workshops and lectures, and there is a guild library.

BIBLIOGRAPHY

The following books are concerned mostly with knitting technique and traditions.

Rae Compton. *Traditional Knitting* (Batsford, 1983)

Sarah Don. *Fairisle Knitting* (Mills and Boon, 1979)

Harmony Guides to Knitting Stitches (3 volumes) (Lyric Books). Useful dictionaries illustrating a wide range of stitches

Cynthia Gravelle LeCount. *Andean Folk Knitting* (Dos Tejedoras Fiber Arts Publications, 1990)

Frances Hinchcliffe. *Knit one, Purl one: Historic and Contemporary Knitting from the V & A's Collection* (Precision Press, London)

Sheila McGregor. *Traditional Fairisle Knitting* (Batsford, 1981)

Sheila McGregor. *Traditional Scandinavian Knitting* (Batsford, 1983)

James Norbury. *Traditional Knitting Patterns* (Dover Publications)

Richard Rutt. *A History of Hand Knitting* (Batsford, 1987)

Montse Stanley. *Knitting (your own designs for a perfect fit)* (David & Charles, 1982)

Montse Stanley. *The Handknitter's Handbook* (David & Charles, 1986). A comprehensive, easy-to-follow book on knitting technique

Mary Thomas's Knitting Book (Hodder and Stoughton, 1938). Another useful, clear book on technique

Mary Thomas's Book of Knitting Patterns (Hodder and Stoughton, 1943)

Gladys Thompson. *Guernsey and Jersey Patterns* (Batsford, 1969)

Barbara Walker. *Treasury of Knitting Patterns* and *Second Treasury of Knitting Patterns* (Scribners USA)

Mary Wright. *Cornish Guernseys and Knit Frocks* (Alison Hodge/Ethnographica, 1979)

ACKNOWLEDGEMENTS

Many people have helped to make this book possible, both directly and indirectly. It began with my mother, who taught me to knit in spite of my persistence in knitting left-handed; she was later followed by art college tutors, who introduced me to fibres, yarns, cloth, dyes and textiles from around the world. More recently, working with students has stimulated a purpose and direction for this book – and then there are my knitters, who patiently knit my designs beautifully and from whom I have learnt a great deal.

Thanks for help with the text go to my father and my editor; for their skill and sympathetic interpretation; to my photographer and illustrator; and for their support, tolerance and encouragement, to my family.

The author and publishers would also like to thank the following for their invaluable help in loaning items or providing photographs for reproduction in this book:

The Institute of Agricultural History and Museum of English Rural Life, University of Reading (photo p8); Guildford Museum, for help with photography (p10); Susan Bosence for the loan of her guernsey; West Surrey College of Art and Design Textile department and Ella Mcleod for the loan of items (photos pp16 and 53); Sarah Burnett (photo p26 by David Burnett); Susan Duckworth (photo p 46 by Sandra Lousada, from Susan Duckworth's *Floral Knitting*, Century); Carole Wainwright for the loan of her jumpers; Yoshimi Kihara (photo p71).

INDEX

Page numbers in *italic* indicate illustrations